LIVING *with* TIGERS

BOOKS BY VALMIK THAPAR
Winged Fire: A Celebration of Indian Birds
Saving Wild India: A Blueprint for Change
Wild Fire: The Splendours of India's Animal Kingdom
Tiger Fire: 500 Years of the Tiger in India
Tiger: Portrait of a Predator
Tigers: The Secret Life
The Tiger's Destiny
The Land of the Tiger: A Natural History of the Indian Subcontinent
The Secret Life of Tigers
Tiger
Wild Tigers of Ranthambhore
Bridge of God: 20 Days in the Masai Mara
The Cult of the Tiger
Tiger: The Ultimate Guide
The Last Tiger
The Illustrated Tigers of India
Ranthambhore: 10 Days in the Tiger Fortress
Tigers and the Banyan Tree
An African Diary: 12 Days in Kenya's Magical Wilderness
The Tiger: Soul of India
Tigers, My Life: Ranthambhore and Beyond
Tigers in the Emerald Forest: Ranthambhore after the Monsoon
My Life with Tigers

BOOKS CO-AUTHORED BY VALMIK THAPAR
With Tigers in the Wild with Fateh Singh Rathore and Tejbir Singh
Tigers and Tigerwallahs with Jim Corbett, Billy Arjan Singh, Geoffrey C. Ward and
Diane Raines Ward
Exotic Aliens with Romila Thapar and Yusuf Ansari

BOOKS EDITED BY VALMIK THAPAR
Saving Wild Tigers, 1900-2000: The Essential Writings
Battling for Survival

LIVING *with* TIGERS

VALMIK THAPAR

SKETCHES BY ROSE CORCORAN

ALEPH

ALEPH

ALEPH BOOK COMPANY
An independent publishing firm
promoted by Rupa Publications India

First published in India in 2016
by Aleph Book Company
7/16 Ansari Road, Daryaganj
New Delhi 110 002

ISBN: 978-93-84067-50-2

1 3 5 7 9 10 8 6 4 2

This book is dedicated to
My son Hamir Thapar whose engagement with the wildlife of Africa and India is
enthralling. I hope his experiences in the future are as engaging
as mine have been.
And
My nephew Jaisal Singh who not only shared some of these encounters but continues
to find ways to engage with the wilderness in India and Africa.
We all must strive to connect good innovative strategies in India and Africa in order to
keep these amazing areas safe.

CONTENTS

AUTHOR'S NOTE

I FIRST CAME UNDER THE TIGER'S SPELL FIFTY-FOUR years ago, at the age of ten, sitting astride an elephant in Corbett National Park in the Lower Himalayas of north India. It was early in the morning and ten elephants were sweeping through high grass in an attempt to spring some tigers into a clearing on the far side. I remember looking down from my perch and seeing a tigress snarling up at the elephant and then darting away with two large cubs at her heels. I was struck by that experience and continue to remember it vividly. It was thirteen years after this encounter that I saw my next tiger in Ranthambhore. The year was 1976. That was the year my life with tigers truly began.

This book is not only about my favourite tigers but also the very best of my encounters with one of the most magnificent animals to walk the face of the planet. Over the past forty years I have tried to serve them as best as I could. It was a dream for me to publish my first book nearly thirty-five years ago and to share my experiences with tigers with people across the world. This is my thirtieth publication and I have loved every minute of my time as an author. Through my books I have shared some of the best photographs showing the diversity of tigers in the wild. This time around I have used only a bunch of sketches. I have to thank Rose Corcoran for her brilliant sketches.

My Ranthambhore journey would not have been

possible without Fateh Singh Rathore, the wildlife warden, welcoming me into the folds of the park. He was not just my tiger mentor but my closest friend. Many of the encounters with the tigers that I describe in the following pages took place when I was with him; he was, in a myriad ways, responsible for my life with tigers. Former Prime Minister Rajiv Gandhi always referred to him as Fateh Singh Ranthambhore. His warmth and generosity of spirit were infectious. He invited me to another home under the canopy of Ranthambhore's forests thus changing my life forever. He inspired many who today fight endless battles to keep wild tigers alive. When he passed away a few years ago he left a void in my life. I miss him sorely and know he will be a presence in my life until the end of my days.

Valmik Thapar
August 2016
New Delhi

THE TIGERS OF RANTHAMBHORE

RANTHAMBHORE TIGER RESERVE IN RAJASTHAN HAS been the root of all my learning throughout my life. It still is. It is within the folds of this forest that I discovered the secrets of the tiger and have had my favourites among these majestic animals over the past forty years. This is the story of the tigers that I befriended and became close to—not just physically but also emotionally. But before I write about them, I should describe the setting in which I worked with them. This setting changed my life in many ways. The best way to recreate it is from my impressions of it forty years ago.

◆

Late one afternoon, in early 1976, I boarded a train for the small town of Sawai Madhopur, a place that was totally unknown to me. I was a city boy and unsure of what lay ahead. All I knew was that I had to get out of Delhi. I had heard of Ranthambhore through my work on various documentary films but could not have imagined then that I would find the lure of the jungle irresistible. All I knew at that time, at the age of twenty-three, was that something was missing in my life. There was a sense of emptiness and despair and a lack of excitement. I needed a break. I remember that that train journey was one of the most difficult that I have ever taken. Instinctively, I must have known that my life was about to change. I watched the dusty plains rush past as the train sped on and soon it was pitch dark. When I disembarked at 10 p.m., I found myself at a station that was dark and deserted. I somehow managed to wake up the driver of a horse carriage that was standing outside. In those days Sawai Madhopur did not boast many jeeps or motorized vehicles. We trotted off to the only hotel nearby—the Maharaja Lodge—where I had to wake the watchman who took his own sweet time to open up a room festooned with cobwebs for me. I spent a sleepless night. The next morning I set off for a walk and was surprised to see that there was no sign of a forest nearby. This was a sleepy district town sprawled untidily around the railway track, which seemed to be the only reason for its existence. I walked around amidst hooting train sounds and felt people staring at me. I must have seemed like an alien. I began to wonder whether there really were any tigers in the area. Soon I found another horse cart that would take me to the office of Project Tiger. The office turned out to be a dismal building in the middle of a mess of concrete and brick that is the mark of every small town in India. A cement factory nearby belched out dirty smoke. Could this be the base for a tiger reserve?

I introduced myself to Fateh Singh Rathore, the wildlife warden of the park, at the barrack-like office. He looked like someone straight out of the American Wild West with his luxuriant moustache and Stetson. I asked his permission to spend some time in the park and he looked me up and down as if I was mad. He told me that no one came there to 'visit' and that I would have to find a jeep and get my rations if I was to stay inside. Not expecting this, I grew a little anxious, but a few hours later I managed to hire a jeep and borrowed Fateh's driver Prahlad to set off for the park. The rations had been bought and I had also taken a crate of Coca-Cola along. At the time Coke was my favourite drink.

Leaving the town we followed a narrow tarred road that ran parallel to a range of hills and after several kilometres turned off onto a dirt track. Slowly the wilderness started taking over and the forest thickened. Suddenly, we were skimming along the rim of a deep ravine, bouncing and jolting over a stony track. In front of us loomed an ancient massive stone gate that must have once been flanked by fortress walls, long since crumbled. It was the royal entrance to Ranthambhore, constructed to protect the domain of kings and surviving today to protect a treasure of equal if not greater value. Centuries ago it must have prevented armies from invading this kingdom. Water flowed down the edge of the gate from a marble cow's head encompassed by a Shivling. A pool of water full of slithery water snakes had formed below the gate; as we moved beyond it the air cooled and the vegetation changed. So did the sounds, as the chatter of birds mixed incongruously with the groan of the jeep. It is truly amazing how birds are able to survive wherever there is a patch of forest and fill our senses with their song. Cresting a rise we saw Ranthambhore Fort, grey and massive, extending upwards from a steep cliff face. The sky was a clear blue, the surrounding forest a dull green just turning to yellow. The huge walls glinted in the evening sunlight, looking for all the world as if man had decided to chisel a bit of nature out of the upper fringe of the rock, rather than disturb or fight it.

The fort was vital for the control of central India and the great Mughal Emperor Akbar laid siege to it in the sixteenth century. In fact, he camped at the fort for a year before taking control. During that time, there are records of battles and intrigue and the politics of the warring groups but no record of hunts. But I am sure Akbar hunted in the plains with his cheetahs racing after herds of blackbuck. It is likely that tigers were also hunted. It is said that, during Akbar's time, one of the unusual ways to hunt tigers was by riding a big male buffalo towards it and then controlling the buffalo such that it tossed the tiger to the ground with its horns. Another unconventional method described is that of tying a bait on a path regularly used by tigers and pouring strong glue around the bait. The tiger would then get stuck to the ground and would lose its energy in the struggle to free himself from the glue. But the greatest tiger story from Emperor Akbar's time is one that is considered one of his miracles. He confronted a tiger and looked at it so ferociously that it submitted in front of the Emperor, turned, and ran away!

I wish I could find a record of the wildlife of the area at that time. Did lions and tigers share this habitat? Did it have cheetahs? I know that Sherpur, a village close to which I have a home, finds mention in Akbar's records as a place where important battles took place, and the area is full of old ruins, revealing its rich history. In the *Akbarnama* there is a superb description of the area from the sixteenth century (1569). It states:

> 'After traversing various stages, H. M. [His Majesty] the Shahinshah reached Rantanbhor—this fort is in the middle of hill country. Hence they say that all other forts are naked, while this is "mail-clad". The real name of the fort is Rantahpur, and Ran is the name of a high

hill which overtops it. On this account the fort has got this name. The fort is very lofty and strong, so that the lasso of the imagination cannot reach its battlements, nor the catapult of the fancy be effectual against its high walls.'

Later on, in the *Tuzuk-i-Jahangiri* or *Memoirs of Jehangir* (1620), a falcon hunt is recorded about 14 to 15 kilometres from the fort, an area that must be a part of the tiger reserve today. Also, it is likely that the house in which Jehangir spent the night was close to Jogi Mahal, which I will describe later, or King Hamir's palace inside the fort. It states:

'On Sunday, the 2nd Elahi month of Dai, the royal standards were raised at the fort of Ranthambur. This is one of the great forts of the Indians. On Monday, the 3rd, I went to inspect the fort. There are two hills close to each other. They call one Ran, and the other Thambur. The fort is built on the top of Thambur, and, putting these two names together, they have called it Ranthambur. Although the fort is exceedingly strong, and has plenty of water, the hill of Ran is a specially strong fortress in itself and the capture of the fortress depends upon the possession of this hill—I had intended to pass the night in the fort, and the next day return to camp. As the buildings inside the fort were built after the fashion of the Hindus, and the rooms were without air, and with little space, they did not please me, nor was I disposed to stay there. I saw a bathhouse, which one of the servants of Dastam Khan had built near the wall of the fort. A little garden and a lodging which overlooks the open space is not wanting in space and air, and there is no better place in the whole fort. On the 7th, I marched 5 kos [about 14 km]. I had before this captured a saras with a falcon, but until now I had never seen the hunting of a durna [crane]. As my son Shahjahan had great pleasure in durna hunting with the falcons, and his falcons were well grown, at his request I rode out early in the morning, and caught one durna myself, whilst the falcon my son had on his wrist caught another. Certainly of all good hunting amusements, this is the best.'

In 1765, Mughal Emperor Shah Alam II issued a firman granting Ranthambhore Fort to Sawai Madho Singh of Jaipur, making him the qiledar. A traveller of those times described the fort as being one of the most famous in India, well-protected, completely inaccessible, and concealed in a mountainous region; surrounded on all sides by high ridges, leaving only the thick forest gorges below to serve as entrances and exits as these could be easily defended. Only cannons could blast down the walls and force entry into the fort; the notorious inaccuracy of cannon fire of the time meant that the fort justified its reputation as being unconquerable. Towers and bastions were built into the walls and the natural rock faces, which added to the fortifications. The rocks on the edges of the ridges constituted another disadvantage for an invading army. These fortifications meant that the occupants of Ranthambhore would suffer only if the fort were under siege. That was why Akbar spent a year laying siege to the fort, and this reality is also revealed by the paintings of those times.

A few hundred years ago, Ranthambhore was used as a prison fortress. Prisoners were fed opium and thrown to their deaths from its ramparts.

The forests below were rich with wildlife. Colonel Tod, in 1829, offers one of the earliest descriptions of the geography of the area:

> At Ranthambhore the plateau breaks into lofty ranges, their white summits sparkling in the sun: cragged but not peaked, and preserving the characteristic formation though disunited from the mass. Here, there are no less than seven distinct ranges—Satpara through all of which the Banas has to force a passage to unite with the Chambal. Beyond Ranthambhore, and the whole way from Karauli to the river, is an irregular tableland.

The *Rajputana Gazetteer* of 1870 includes the following description:

> In the wooded glens near the Chambal in the southwest, tigers are so numerous that cattle cannot graze in them without special precautions, and the population of the country must be seriously affected by these destructive beasts. Bears, sambar, nilgai, deer likewise abound in this locality, which would be a paradise for a sportsman.

By the turn of the twentieth century, the forests of Ranthambhore became the private hunting reserves of the maharajas of Jaipur. This probably slowed down the destruction of both the forest and the tiger, as the maharajas' men started protecting them. Shooting was permitted only for special guests. A one-month shooting camp was held in

Sawai Madhopur, and most of the shoots were around the town where the forest spilt over. The hunts are described in great detail by Colonel Kesri Singh in his book, *The Tiger of Rajasthan*. The guests included royalty and nobility from all over Europe, and a number of maharajas from all over India. Kesri Singh managed the shoots well without depleting the forests. The last major shoot was held for the Queen of England and the Duke of Edinburgh in 1961.

◆

I thought about everything I had read about Ranthambhore as we began to wind our way up the road that ran along the right flank of the fort. The forest had grown very dense. We would soon be at our destination. I strained to see through the trees for signs of wildlife, but my eyes were not yet accustomed to seeing in the forest. I did not know then that it would take years for that skill to develop. I could see old peepul trees and large banyans and I wondered how much they had changed since Ranthambhore's glory days. As we crested another rise the terrain changed dramatically. The steep hills gave way to a broad valley dotted with low hills and a large expanse of water clothed entirely in giant pink and white lotuses. The colour of the blooms resembled the pink of lotus flowers that dotted the cloth paintings or Pichhwais from the area of Nathdwara near Udaipur, a pink that I had never before believed possible to encounter in real life. It was too much to assimilate all at once, this mix of history, man and nature.

As we branched to the left I thought we were plunging into the largest banyan tree I had ever seen. Two of its hundreds of roots formed a natural gateway to Jogi Mahal, the forest rest house, which decades ago had been the residence of a temple priest. Before the driver could even stop I raced up the steps across a wide terrace and through a high arched doorway to an awe-inspiring view. There at my feet lay the lake of lotuses that I had glimpsed earlier, with the waters of the lake lapping peacefully against the base of the rest house. In the distance crocodiles lay sunbathing, one with its jaw open, another gliding lazily through the water. Wild boar, chital and sambar fed on the lush grass on the bank of the lake. Some of the sambar were half immersed in the water nibbling at the lotus leaves. Darters, herons, grebes and kingfishers were flying around in abandon. Occasionally a large fish would breach the surface of the lake and fall back into the water with a loud slapping noise. To the right of the lake were the remnants of an old masjid and upon the opposite hill was an ancient guard post. On the other side were the vast banyan tree and the backdrop of Ranthambhore Fort, which filled the horizon with its imposing presence. It was a moment of hypnotic intensity for me and I was suddenly exhausted. This is where I would stay. I did not know then that Ranthambhore would become more like home over the next forty years and a place that would always regenerate my soul.

Jogi Mahal was simply appointed without the fuss or garishness of modern lodges. There was no electricity and modernization was far away.

Soon the forest staff gathered around me—the tiger tracker Laddu, the wireless operator Ramu, the driver Prahlad, and the forest guard and caretaker of the rest house Badhyaya. As the chill of the night descended, we lit a fire.

The crackling of firewood mingled with the sounds of the night. Crickets, nightjars and owls had woken up to the dark. Small bats whizzed around and a large flying fox flapped above us. I was in another world. Laddu held forth about tigers and their activity at night and Ramu talked of all the ghosts that had been left behind from the wars that had ravaged the area. Prahlad added that there were even a few spears embedded in the walls. Suddenly a loud booming sound shattered the night, making me jump. My forest friends laughed and told me it was the alarm call of the sambar.

It was in this pitch darkness that I had my greatest lessons about the language of the forest. Unused to life in the open I would take fright at the slightest sound but I slowly began to learn that these sounds indicated the presence of predators be they tigers or leopards. Each deer and antelope had different alarm calls that warned others of approaching danger. A predator was on the prowl and the tension in the air was palpable. Those nocturnal alarm calls were shrill and echoed off the ramparts of the fort. Each time we heard them torches were flashed around the roots of the banyan tree in the hope of seeing a leopard if not a tiger. It became a dream of mine to one day photograph a tiger walking around this massive tree. It would be more than thirty-five years before this dream could come true. Sambar calls were considered a confirmation of the presence of either tiger or leopard and the frequency of calls indicated the movement of the animal.

In the years that followed I would learn the finer nuances of these sounds which would play a vital part in my search for tigers. But during those first few days they were

my introduction to this wonderful forest and its magical aura. Ranthambhore began entering my bloodstream and those first twenty days were memorable as I was initiated into a new world. There were animal tracks in the morning that told you the stories of the night. You had to be like a jungle detective looking for clues of tigers that had walked past, or leopards and porcupines that had crossed, or drag marks where small and large animals had been killed and dragged into cover to be fed on. In those early days just seeing the tiger's pug marks was a source of celebration.

There were still villages everywhere and human disturbance was high. Parts of the forest were under agriculture and the occasional bullock cart would travel along the jeep tracks.

During my first days in Ranthambhore, I felt I was shedding one layer of skin and putting on another. I would spend hours walking to the lake palace at Rajbagh to watch the birds, crocodiles and deer. It was a gem in the heart of the forest with sweeping expanses of water on each side. Lotus flowers both pink and white filled the edges and this was like an earthly paradise. Locals believed that the area was full of ghosts and once when I was filming some sequences there in 1976, we accidentally left our sound recordist behind in the ruins. He told us later that he heard music and saw shadowy figures that enveloped him. Even though his record button was on nothing got recorded. When my jeep went to pick him up he was in a cold sweat, shivering from the shock. The spirits had possessed him and he only recovered when a local used seven chillies to draw out the spirits! I did not know then that in years to come this palace would become the den of all the lake tigers and few humans would set foot inside.

Ranthambhore Fort dominated the landscape. It was several kilometres in circumference and dotted with ruins and palaces, lakes and ponds. As I have mentioned earlier, it figured prominently in the rich history of northern India and a few spears from bygone battles are still embedded in the walls. The views from each corner are spectacular and you can get a bird's-eye view of the lakes and of a thick gorge on the far side with the rolling hills of the Aravallis in the background. One of the forest guards told me that it is the haunt of leopards that even walk on the walls. Tigers frequent it less as there are too many pilgrims who go up and down seeking the blessings of Lord Ganesh. There is a great sense of infinity at the top and a serene and eerie silence as you look down from the ramparts. In the years that followed I saw tigers several times from the top as they walked the lakes. The day before my departure was when I had my first tiger experience in Ranthambhore. As I have said in the Author's Note, my first experience of wild tigers was when I was ten in Corbett National Park. Thirteen years later, in Ranthambhore, the tiger was nearly invisible even though its pug marks were visible in the day. It was a challenge to spot a tiger. In those days male buffalo were tied to trees as bait to attract the tiger but by the morning there were few signs of the predator. The tiger either dragged its victim away or was so cautious that it did not even approach to kill it. On the nineteenth day of my stay Badhyaya had tied three baits in different areas. After an early dinner I took off with Prahlad in the jeep. With searchlight in hand we arrived within minutes at Singh Dwar only to find the buffalo was down. A leopard was nibbling nervously at the carcass. It was my first glimpse of a Ranthambhore leopard and I was taking the sight in when suddenly the loud booming alarm calls of the sambar exploded and the leopard jumped up and darted across our path before clambering up a banyan tree. He then waited patiently. Prahlad was convinced that a tiger had made the kill but being shy had moved off to wait. The leopard had taken advantage of the moment to scavenge but had been frightened off by the proximity of the alarm calls. The tension mounted as we waited. But nothing happened. Prahlad was sure the tiger would not show while we were there. Thirty minutes later we moved off to the second site at Mori near Rajbagh Lake. Again the buffalo was gone. Prahlad and I tried very hard to negotiate the terrain around an old wall that prevented visibility. Suddenly my searchlight found its target. A huge tiger's head filled the night. I nearly dropped the light. The face was there for a few seconds but then it vanished. I had to rub my eyes to check whether this was a mirage or reality. This magical appearing and disappearing trick is the tiger's speciality. I quickly realized that this was an opportunity of a lifetime and rushed off to bring Fateh back from Sawai Madhopur half an hour away. I knew the tiger would continue feeding and maybe Fateh's expertise would come in handy.

I had met Fateh a few times over the past weeks and we were getting to know each other slowly. When I arrived at his house at 11 p.m. I found him having a drink. He agreed to join me, jumped into the jeep and we drove back at a furious pace. As soon as we arrived Fateh went into action, drove the jeep up an incline and we ended up with a snarling tiger in front of us. I had never experienced such excitement as I did at that moment. As it neared midnight Fateh decided that he could get us to an even better vantage point but while negotiating a few rocks he drove straight into the lake. I could not believe it—there we were, stuck in the water, with the tiger only metres away. Luckily the wireless radio was working and Fateh summoned another jeep to pull us out. The jeep came to our rescue an hour later but the noise had frightened the tiger away. In later years I would experience many more tiger encounters along with Fateh but at that time it was the most exciting day of my life.

I was due to leave the next morning. I was sad but knew that I would be back soon. What had been so special about my visit was that this place had given me peace, real peace. No rules and regulations, only one tourist in twenty days and a freedom to explore that I had never experienced in my life. I knew deep down that my life had changed forever. When I look back it is very clear to me that I fell in love first with Ranthambhore's enchanting forests, which encompassed the memories of man. This was no ordinary forest. It was dotted everywhere with the crumbling ruins of a historic past. History and natural history merged together and in this setting I once again fell in love with the tiger. Would my life have been different if the setting were different? Would I have spent forty years on the trail of the tiger outside of Ranthambhore? Probably not.

◆

This book is about my experiences and observations over forty years. Still under the spell of my first visit to Ranthambhore, I began to read and learn more about the majestic striped big cat known as the tiger or *Panthera tigris*. Tigris—the species name that differentiates the tiger from the other members of the Panthera genus or group, namely *Panthera leo* (lion), *Panthera pardus* (leopard) and *Panthera onca* (jaguar)—is classical Greek for 'arrow', from which both the straight and fast-flowing river Tigris and the speedy tiger get their names. The origins of the tiger date back nearly fifty million years, long before anything recognizable as today's big cats existed. Fossils provide most of the evidence scientists and researchers have used to piece together our understanding of the emergence of the tiger. When we fast forward to more recent times the record books of the nineteenth and twentieth centuries reveal that the tiger population suffered unprecedented decimation when the proliferation of firearms and cars facilitated hunting for sport or medicinal purposes. People also hunted the tiger's prey, leaving tigers with less and less to eat. Humankind encroached upon the tiger's natural habitats, converting them to agricultural lands. In the fifty years between 1875 and 1925, 80,000 tigers were killed in India alone. Probably an equal number were injured and died later of their wounds. Based on these and other figures it is conservatively estimated that at the dawn of the twentieth century 100,000 tigers inhabited the range from eastern Turkey across the

Asian continent to Russia, the Far East and the islands of Indonesia.

For centuries sportsmen and naturalists have tried to get close to tigers but rarely does this elusive predator oblige. It has been hunted, injured and disturbed so much that it instinctively keeps away from man. The challenge ahead of me was enormous. In 1976 very little was known about wild tigers. Based on my experience of nearly forty years I have to admit that observing tigers in the wild must surely be one of the most time-consuming activities in the field of natural history. It requires infinite patience and perseverance— not only when the tiger is nowhere to be found but even when he is right there in front of you. And the reason is very simple. Like most hunters, and especially the larger ones, the tiger spends most of its twenty-four-hour cycle resting; always watchful, ever alert but conserving its energy. Even after watching a tiger for six hours without a break you would count yourself lucky to see a few minutes of exciting action. For 80 per cent of the time the tiger sits or sleeps; dozing in a shady strategically placed spot in the day, occasionally getting up to stretch or to watch a group of deer or peacocks pass by in the distance. Early morning and late evening are times for grooming, and the tiger will spend much time licking its paws, chest and back getting ready to walk across his territory.

When it is very hot tigers will stroll to a stream or waterhole for a soak and a drink. For 10 per cent of the time that they are awake they walk on man-made paths and animal tracks hoping to bump into prey and at the same time patrol their areas. The remaining 10 per cent of their 'awake time' constitutes everything enthralling about the tiger's life and it is this that I will describe in detail.

After that first memorable visit my trips to Ranthambhore became more frequent and I slowly shed my Delhi life that included a marriage gone wrong and my work as a documentary film-maker. Ranthambhore and tigers became my full-time focus and obsession. The forest was extraordinary and utterly striking as it changed from season to season. Lush and green after the monsoon with gushing waterfalls and gurgling streams, changing to a golden russet colour in the winter as the nutritious leaves of the dhok trees begin to fall and the forest looks totally bare, then turning from yellow to green in the spring. By the early summer a variety of vegetation covers the forest floor and the flame of the forest begins to bloom, turning large patches of forest a vivid red. The forest then waits for the skies to open to welcome the monsoon but if it rains in the winter or spring for more than a few hours the dhok tree goes green all over again.

Before I get down to describing my experiences with the wild tigers I have spent practically all my adult life with I reckon it would interest the reader to know why each of them features in the book.

I start with Padmini, whom I describe as the queen mother, a tigress who was calm, mature and intelligent. I studied her as she raised her cubs. Akbar and Babur were the most curious and confident of the litter but my favourite was Laxmi (of whom more later) the smallest, and weakest of the lot.

The next tiger which makes an appearance in the book is Genghis, the master predator, who was a regular sight around the lakes of Ranthambhore. He had mastered the art of killing sambars in the water, the first time this form of tiger predation had been observed anywhere in the world.

Genghis is followed by Noon, one of my all-time favourites. She earned her name because rather unusually she was at her most active in the middle of the day. Noon learned the art of killing prey in the water from Genghis.

I then write about Broken Tooth, a big male with a gentle nature, whom I observed for ten years between 1979 and 1989.

It also gave me great joy to get to know Laxmi, Padmini's daughter. She was an exceptional mother and it was a joy to see the special bond she shared with her three cubs.

Then there was Machli, a star turn for all those who visited the park. Sadly, she died in August when this book was going to press, but holds the record for the longest lived wild tiger in the world.

Over the last decade, the practice of naming the wild tigers of Ranthambhore was phased out and they began to be identified by numbers. I write about T24, an unpredictable tiger popularly known as Ustad. Other tigers who feature in the book include T17 and T19.

Over the years I must have observed and recorded the behaviour of at least 125 tigers in Ranthambhore. But the tigers you will find in the pages of this book are the special ones, the ones who taught me everything I know about tigers, the ones who, by letting me into their lives, made my own life truly worth living.

PADMINI—THE QUEEN MOTHER

WHEN I FIRST WENT TO RANTHAMBHORE IN EARLY 1976, seeing wild tigers was the most difficult of tasks. You could roam the forest for days and nights without ever encountering even a sign of a tiger. If we saw a fresh pug mark it was a moment to celebrate and a glimpse of a tiger even for a second was like witnessing a wonder of the world. The park then was full of villages and bullock carts that plied the tracks. Agricultural fields dotted the landscape and even near Jogi Mahal a crop field surrounded the huge banyan tree. There were no tourists and no rules. Our first glimpses of tigers were always at night and the tiger was completely nocturnal, keeping far away from the daytime activities of man. Therefore, to encounter a tiger I had to lead a nocturnal life sleeping most of the day and waking at sunset to explore this land of the tiger. Most of the night and sometimes until dawn we would criss-cross the forest waiting for the alarm calls of deer to signal the movement of tigers. At the most, once or twice a month, we would feel excited and exhilarated as a tiger would flash across the road, caught momentarily in our jeep's headlights. These sightings lasted only for a few seconds and we had to rub our eyes in disbelief to absorb what we had seen. Most of 1976 rolled by in this way and I slowly got to know and trust Fateh, who became my tiger guru. We became good friends and our friendship lasted for thirty-five years.

The period 1976-77 was a busy one for Fateh. He was in the midst of shifting and resettling villages as part of an enormous effort to prevent human disturbance in the core area of the park. My first trips to the park were full of encounters with village carts and people moving from Berda to Lakarda to the Ranthambhore Fort and then back up to Anantpura. Crops grew on the edges of the lake of Jogi Mahal, and Ranthambhore Fort boasted a village at its base. Lakarda and Lahpur were full of human activity and there was not a scent of a tiger for miles. Today all these places are the best locations for wild tigers. Fateh always said that tigers and people cannot coexist and until the villages were resettled tigers would never come into their own. He believed that this was the single most important mission to breathe life into Ranthambhore and from 1976–79 he resettled twelve villages. He was convinced that this process alone would put Ranthambhore on the world map for tigers and make it a prime destination for viewing them. He firmly believed that once the fear of man was removed the tiger would shed its nocturnal habit for a more diurnal one. I would argue about this but in the end he was proved right. Ranthambhore began to change and in those early years, tiger sightings increased proportionally to the villages being resettled. On my third trip to Ranthambhore in 1976 the village of Lakarda had gone and the entire area had started regenerating with new grass following the monsoon. The deer and antelope were back. Herds of nilgai or blue bulls grazed on the fresh grass.

It was at the end of the first year that we became aware of the regular presence of a tigress around Jogi Mahal and in an area of 45 square kilometres up to Lakarda and Berda. We had never seen her. Tigers then were very shy and ran off if they detected the slightest human presence or the sound of a jeep. But Fateh was hopeful that one day the tigress's pug marks would be accompanied by those of her little ones. I never thought that I would have the privilege of seeing the pug marks of cubs but Fateh was an optimist. He even believed that with cubs we would actually have a better chance of seeing the mother.

Early in 1977, while I was in Delhi, I got a telegram. 'Come soon. Tigress with five cubs spotted.' I couldn't believe it. There were few records of a tigress with five cubs from anywhere on the planet. I immediately made plans to leave for Ranthambhore. When I arrived at Sawai Madhopur station early that afternoon I found a jeep waiting for me. Fateh's driver Prahlad informed me that the boss was sitting on a tree looking at a tigress. We sped off to find him. When we reached Lakarda we found a beaming Fateh sprawled across a branch of a tree. Bursting with excitement, he slowly made his way down the branches. He had been watching a tigress and her five five-month old cubs in thick bush as they feasted on a buffalo that had turned feral, left behind by the villagers of Lakarda after their resettlement. He had already given the tigress a name—Padmini, after his daughter. Padmini was a slender and elegant tigress—her pale colour was offset by very calm eyes that seldom turned angry. She was rarely ruffled by anything. Because she was so easy and relaxed in the presence of humans all her cubs developed the same trait. This was then passed on to new generations of tigers in Ranthambhore.

The next day I had my first glimpse of Padmini from the jeep as she dragged away the remnants of a carcass into thicker bush. I will never forget that moment with Padmini. It was the first time in nearly a year that I had seen a tiger in daylight hours. Tears of joy rolled down my face and I knew this was only the beginning of a lifelong engagement that would be all-consuming in my life. Ten days later, in the same area at dawn, we heard a cacophony of sambar alarm calls coming from deep in a valley. Fateh suggested that we crawl to the edge of the hill to see what was going on in the valley below. We left the jeep and crawled for a hundred metres. As we looked down we saw Padmini walking across the Lakarda grassland followed by her five cubs. She glanced upwards and saw us on the skyline but we were lucky to see the entire family for a full minute. Short glimpses like this over the next month and we knew for sure that there were three male and two female cubs in the litter. We gave them names. The males became Akbar, Babur and Hamir; the females Laxmi and Begum. Akbar was the most confident and curious of the five cubs and clearly the dominant cub of the litter, followed by Babur and Hamir. Laxmi spent most of her time following her mother's every step and little Begum was the shyest and also the last to eat as her siblings would push her away at a kill. We worried that Begum might not survive. A brood of five is very rare amongst tigers and she was getting the least to eat. A month later our worst fears were realized. Begum was no more. Nature had eased her out.

At this time in Ranthambhore live baits of small buffalo were used regularly by the park management to sight tigers and to record tiger numbers. Fateh decided that this was an opportunity to see Padmini and her family for longer spells, so baits were placed once a week for two months depending on Padmini's whereabouts. I was under tiger training and my job was to walk out at dusk with the tracker Badhyaya and a bait and tie it wherever the tiger's presence was the freshest.

During these risk-laden journeys on foot Badhyaya and I became very close and I learnt much from his instinctive knowledge of the language of the forest. He remained my favourite forest guard until his death in the mid-1990s. Slim and diminutive he had no fear of tigers. One evening Fateh said to me, 'Let's see how fearless you are.' At about 10 p.m., after a couple of drinks, we got into a jeep and Fateh told Badhyaya to load a small buffalo in the back of the vehicle. He then turned to me and said, 'If we find Padmini you are going to pull this buffalo out and tie it to a tree in front of her.' My heart thudded in panic. I did not come from a 'buffalo tying in front of a tiger' background or family. But with Fateh you could never say no. I remember breaking out in a sweat and wishing we would never encounter Padmini. But no such luck and soon in the valley of Nalghati the searchlight encountered a row of glinting eyes. There, dazzling us, was Padmini with her four cubs, now nearly eleven months old. Fateh turned off the engine of the jeep and the lights. Silence and darkness descended. The buffalo groaned and Padmini knew that a feast awaited her. Fateh literally pushed me out of the jeep and asked Badhyaya to push out the buffalo and hand me the rope with which it was tied. He turned the light on to the trunk of a tree and told me to tie the rope to the trunk. I saw Padmini watching us intently from 40 feet away. Paralysed by fear, I stumbled forward in a stupor and tied the buffalo to the tree trunk and fled back into the jeep where Fateh had the searchlight focused on Padmini. She was already stalking the buffalo, her muscles rippling. When the buffalo saw the tigress it freed itself with a great pull of the rope. In my panic I must have tied a loose knot. As the buffalo fled Padmini raced in and walloped it, disabling its rear leg. Not only was Fateh training me to lose my fear of the tiger, but Padmini seemed to be training her cubs in the art of hunting. Padmini went and lay down behind a bush. Akbar and Babur moved in. For thirty minutes the three-legged buffalo defended himself valiantly, charging the two young tigers who kept retreating. It was fascinating to watch. It was like boxers in a ring sparring without touching each other. Then suddenly Akbar leapt on the buffalo forcing it to the ground and struggled with it—much like a wrestler—until he finally found a grip on the neck. Babur joined the fray and jumped on the hindquarters. The buffalo died a slow death. The cubs had much to learn. Soon they were feasting but after about forty minutes Padmini came up and coughed at them, forcing them to retreat. Then Hamir slowly made his way to the kill followed by Laxmi. Padmini controlled the feeding carefully. In between she helped herself. I was watching mesmerized and all fear of tigers had vanished. The hours rolled by. In front of us the secret lives of tigers were unfolding. In the next months as the cubs grew their feeding would be closely managed by their mother so that each cub ate alone, the first feeder being the most dominant. This prevented aggression and conflict amongst the cubs.

Most of my nights were spent watching the cubs in the Nalghati Valley. Many of these were full moon nights that made the scene around surreal. Silver, bluish light struck the forest and reflected off the tiger's coat. Where in the world could you find this kind of natural beauty? How many had the opportunity to soak it in? I lived as if in a dream. Padmini would go off and leave the cubs sprawled on the black rocks on the slopes of the hills. I used to watch them with a searchlight and a torch waiting expectantly for first light and a glimpse of them before they moved upwards. Akbar, the dominant male cub, would jump on these rocks to pose for us and get really close. The rest would watch from a little distance above. The setting was splendid and I got what I then considered were unique portraits of these young ones as they draped the black rocks of Nalghati. They were still basically nocturnal and wanted to vanish from our presence at first light but slowly each day they would spend a little more time watching us. Even forty years later, Nalghati is a place I frequently visit and play back incredible memories of those unforgettable times.

I think of 1977 and 1978 as the Padmini years during which we played a game of hide-and-seek with her. Our observations increased as the family slowly became comfortable in our presence. They were becoming less elusive and evasive and were shedding their nocturnal cloak just like a snake sheds its skin. This change indicated that they were reposing their trust in those who managed these areas. Padmini was a most devoted mother and was now hunting non-stop to feed the ever growing appetite of her cubs. Her dominant cub Akbar was the most curious and always approached us first. He was also the last to leave in the mornings. He was easily recognizable, with a V-shaped mark on his cheek, and was fearless compared to his siblings. He initially associated the jeep with buffalo and food, but Fateh had slowly phased out baits from the diet as the months went by. There were plenty of night excursions to look for Padmini and her cubs and on one of these we encountered four tigers feeding on the remnants of a spotted deer. We watched them with a searchlight that was connected to the jeep's battery. Fateh did not realize that the battery was getting discharged. When we were ready to go the jeep did not start. Fateh tried everything but in vain. Finally, he suggested that we walk back. We were 2 kilometres from Jogi Mahal. With our hearts in our mouths, the four of us left the jeep in pitch darkness with tigers just 20 feet away and feeding. Fateh told us not to look back and sang film songs and ghazals for more than a half hour until we arrived at Jogi Mahal. It was an experience that I can summon up effortlessly to this day. Tigers lurking in the shadows behind us and Fateh singing, 'Yeh raaten, yeh mausam, yeh hasna hasana, mujhe na bhulna bhulana?' But it was experiences such as this one that helped in my understanding of tigers. Our challenge was to watch the family over a natural kill in full daylight, something that we had never seen until then. It happened one day late in 1977 in the Semli Valley when we pulled over on a grassy verge and found Padmini grooming herself close by. In the grass two cubs were engaged in a tug of war over the remnants of an enormous spotted deer stag. It was our first sighting of them on a natural kill. The male cubs were aggressive and Akbar was at his best, getting the lion's share. Babur and Hamir awaited their turn and even tried a tug of war with the carcass to break it into bits. Laxmi was the calmest, eating last but able to fend off her brothers. Tigers still had memories of man and cowbells—with their association to livestock and food—attracted them. I had a bell in the jeep and one evening in Malik Talao, while waiting for Padmini's cubs, I started ringing it. Nothing happened for a few minutes. Then suddenly Badhyaya, who was sitting next to me, said, 'Tiger.' I got a shock. I was outside the jeep and there was Laxmi approaching us. She was slouched low as if ready to stalk and pounce. I still remember the grass moving under her feet as she paced forward. I clicked a few photographs—they are some of my favourite ones even today—and leapt back into the jeep. She walked around the jeep to check if there was a buffalo inside! On another occasion I was walking in Nalghati looking for a missing bait. We couldn't see either bait or tiger and for some ungodly reason I started ringing the cowbell believing if there was a tiger it would show itself. From a few feet away a tiger leapt out of a ravine and raced over the hill. I stood petrified. The driver later told me that he thought that would be the end of me.

Our tiger sightings at this point came from hard work in the day and sometimes at night to track tigers down. In the light of what happens today the process in 1979 was unbelievable and difficult even to explain to someone who encounters tigers soon after they enter the park and believes that this is the way tigers are. What they don't realize is that it was Fateh's hard work over the years that created the conditions for this to happen.

◆

My encounters with Padmini all those years ago remain etched in my memory and I learnt many lessons from them. In my records of these encounters, I noted that 'tracking a tiger in the wild can be a tense, time-consuming and frustrating experience, but it can also be unbelievably exciting and fulfilling. Sightings during the day are difficult if not impossible, with the lush forest providing the perfect camouflage. Tigers are nocturnal hunters and their "day" begins after sunset. Males, females and cubs come to life under cover of darkness to fraternize, prowl and hunt throughout the forest. The tigers' nocturnal adventure usually begins with a long, cooling drink at a waterhole. While the tigers are just getting started, observers begin to position themselves at vantage points within the forest where the sounds of the forest can be heard over long distances. The alarm calls of peacocks, sambar, chital and blue bulls mingle with the cackling bark of langur monkeys and indicate the presence of tigers, leopards, jackals, hyenas and smaller cats. By following the approximate direction of the sound, one can hazard a guess as to which predator has triggered the alarm. Peacocks can pinpoint the predator's location with amazing accuracy. Occasionally, the clamour raised by the hunted can be a false alarm.

'A careful examination of pug marks will reveal which animal has left the trail. Larger predators tend to stick to man-made paths and animal tracks which suit their soft pads. If you have the good fortune to come across evidence of the presence of a tiger, pinpoint the exact location and keep on the animal's trail. If possible, follow the tracks until dawn, otherwise track the same area at dawn to follow the tiger's night course. This can be a challenging task as tigers can walk from 10 to 18 kilometres in one night and their pug marks may appear and disappear on the trail. On occasion the animal may stray into thicker forest without leaving a trail. The sky can also provide useful clues: hovering vultures or crows could indicate the presence of a possible tiger kill that has been abandoned at daybreak. The kill will provide clues about the attack. If the kill has not been eaten completely, there is a good chance that the tiger will return to finish his meal so you can either bait the animal or find a hideout in the safety of a tree from which to watch at dusk. Extreme caution must be exercised in the vicinity of a kill because the tiger may still be nearby. After a heavy meal tigers tend to take shelter within a radius of a kilometre from the kill. To locate a hidden tiger in the vicinity of a kill, one can follow the tracks on the ground and then look for the nearest thick green cover, dry riverbed or a cool and shady waterhole where the tiger is likely to rest. If the tiger is nearby, it will sense the presence of a human intruder before it is spotted and will most likely vanish silently but it may roar in irritation at being disturbed. People looking for tigers are advised to return to the site of a kill in a jeep. There is probably a 5 to 8 per cent chance of finding a tiger through this process. After searching on foot and by jeep, you might catch a fleeting glimpse of a tiger every twelve or fifteen days. That is why the tiger is called the world's most elusive predator. Tracking is tough especially in the scorching heat of the summer, which is the best time to watch tigers near water. Look for the coolest places. I call them the "air-conditioned" rooms. Even caves and crevices. That is how tigers fight the heat.'

As you track the tiger, the language of the jungle envelopes you. You become alert to the tension in every rustling leaf, in every impression on the ground, as you look and listen to what deceptively appears a silent and deserted forest.

◆

Our life for many months through the year remained unaltered for decades. Slowly everything changed. Tourism raced ahead by the end of the 1980s and in the years that followed Ranthambhore became a 1,800-bed destination. Today the city of Sawai Madhopur is the tiger capital of the world with a turnover of nearly ₹400 crores per year for the local economy. The era of the 1970s today seems like a different world but that is when I learnt the most about jungle law and lore. I remember how difficult it was even to glimpse a male tiger in those early years. We would find pug marks once in two weeks but never the tiger. One day we came across the large pug marks of a male tiger in the Kachida Valley. In our interpretation of pugs the bigger, squarer pug mark was the male, and the more tapering one the female. The male tiger had walked straight down the road from the water of Kachida to Singh Dwar and branched off into a thickly forested riverbed for his day's rest. We kept our fingers crossed that he would move out in the evening. We planned our strategy carefully and decided to wait at the spot where the tiger had branched off. Fateh became restless by 5 p.m. and decided to start ringing the cowbell which he always carried with him to attract tigers (this was before I tried the same trick, which I have described earlier in the book). I laughed and told him it would never work. There we sat for twenty minutes ringing the bell and looking foolish but then suddenly a langur started calling and we drove to the tree where the langurs were in order to see what they were looking at. The calls continued as the langurs scanned a riverbed. And then, lo and behold, we saw a black, tan and white mirage slowly walking towards us. The tiger had been roused by the bell and was passing by to investigate. Twenty feet ahead of us the tiger leapt across the road and looked at us in disdain.

He then paced up the road and sat at the edge. He started grooming himself. His tongue cleaned every crevice as he prepared for his next stroll.

The tiger's rasping tongue is like a comb and removes loose hairs and dirt. As tigers lick themselves, they heal small wounds and cuts. When the tongue cannot reach the wound they wet their paw with saliva and dab the injured area, especially if the injury is around the eyes and head. Cubs will lick their mother's cuts instinctively to help the healing process. The tiger's saliva is the best antiseptic and cleanser. The tongue also has taste buds that can distinguish between bitter and sweet taste. Human tongues have more complex and dense taste buds that are even more discerning. But our saliva is not such a strong antiseptic.

The tiger would move as soon as the last light of the day had gone. A sambar nearby let loose with alarm calls—I counted sixty-seven of them. Peacocks were also calling from their evening perches on trees. We sat in silence until dark. The tiger then rose and came back onto the road and paced on. I looked up at the stars and a new moon. The crickets chirped and nightjars called. From far away I heard the deep call of the brown fishing owl. We followed the tiger for a while and then slowly moved off and went home. When we reached the banyan tree in Jogi Mahal we celebrated with a stiff whisky. We had seen a tiger and that too the very elusive male after twenty days of hard work. It was a red-letter day for us all.

◆

Tigers are very individualistic in their eating habits and over the decades I would watch them feasting over hundreds of kills and observe more than 150 animals being killed. Sambar, nilgai, chital, wild boar were a regular part of the tiger's diet. In most cases death had occurred through a vice-like grip on the throat of the victim. Sometimes the tiger's canines penetrate the jugular vein or the pounce breaks the neck, leading to instant death. This is how big and small cats kill. Death comes quickly to the victim unlike the way hyenas and wild dogs bring down prey, which they start eating while it is still alive. The only time big cats do this is when their prey is large—tigers bringing down an elephant will take chunks out of it alive and so will lions with wild buffalo or giraffes. It is when the neck of the animal is too difficult to clamp on or get to that animals are first disabled and severely mauled. I have never seen a tiger bring down an elephant or rhino or wild buffalo but have watched lions in Africa pounce on a wild buffalo and commence eating it while it was still alive.

Inexperienced tigers are messy killers. They can maul the carcass without cause leaving claw marks and scratches on both neck and rump. Killing techniques are perfected with time. The same is true of slicing and cleaning out the stomach contents. Inexperienced tigers fail to pluck out the stomach causing the carcass to bloat and smell as it remains full of gases. Tigers that are nervous at kills also fail to clean out the stomach. By the time Padmini and her four young ones were finished with a carcass it looked as if it had been bulldozed—just the innards remained with bits of bone scattered around. All the flesh had been consumed, even the edges of the skull. Tigers learn how to eat properly over an extended period of time; they reach perfection by the age of four. Experienced tigers are clean and neat eaters. They can eat every day for five days or eat hugely in one sitting and then desert the carcass leaving behind a feast for the vultures. I have watched a big male tiger all night as he consumed what must have been 35 kilograms of meat in one sitting. As many as seven days can go by in between meals.

◆

By early 1979 Padmini's cubs were sub-adults and both Fateh and I knew the family was getting ready to disperse. Padmini was absent for longer periods from her raucous brood and in her absence Akbar was boss. He had already started killing chital fawns and his siblings were endlessly chasing peafowl. And then by May 1979 there was no sign of Akbar. He had gone to find a life of his own. Two months later Babur and Hamir left. Little Laxmi was the last to leave Padmini in the monsoon of 1979. We knew that within months Padmini would find a mate and hopefully have another litter. It was a time when resident male tigers were impossible to see. They were like ghosts in the forest and our encounters with them were few and far between. Their lives were still a complete secret.

By the end of 1979 the park was less disturbed. Fateh had, in a Herculean feat, managed to resettle twelve villages. The noise of the day had gone and the agricultural fields had turned magically into bush. Bullock carts no longer clattered along the tracks. Peace descended on the forest. Padmini's first litter was dispersing into a habitat free of humans and my fingers were crossed that they would be the first generation of tigers to grow up without fear of man. My own fear of tigers was gone by now and I would walk confidently in the forest by day or by night.

As we headed into 1979 we hoped Padmini would reveal her next litter. We were driving in the upper regions of Rajbagh Lake in December when Fateh suddenly said, 'Tigers.' There, sprawled across some black rocks, was Padmini with a litter of three now looking as if they were three to four months old. She had carefully kept them out of human sight in their first months. Padmini knew us well but her cubs were shy and we had to get them to be comfortable in our presence. Slowly we got closer and closer. Every extra minute you spend makes a difference when it comes to building the trust of the cubs in you. But you have to be patient.

Our patience was rewarded one day when at a turn in the road, we came across Padmini and her new family. She had killed an adult sambar that was too large for her to drag away. It lay close to the road. The entire family was there with the dominant cub playing with the branch of a tree, then patting and rolling a rock, as if it were a football, pawing an insect and even watching a butterfly. The other two cubs remained cautious and in the background. Padmini was closest to the carcass ensuring that no one could scavenge it. The family dozed for a while and then as if on a signal the cubs went out of sight. Soon a bunch of crows fell on the meat but were repeatedly charged by Padmini. Both vultures and crows waited, hoping the tigress would leave. It was hot and at noon we decided to head back to the rest house, leaving Padmini to guard her family's precious food with single-minded dedication.

In the last few years Padmini had added seven tigers to Ranthambhore. The park at this time faced the problem of both poaching and illegal grazing. Animals and wood were both being poached. To protect this tiger turf Fateh had to lead his men from the front. On one occasion in 1981, while driving in the very heart of Padmini's territory in the valley of Lakarda, Fateh unexpectedly came upon a large bunch of graziers all armed with 5-foot lathis. He was so shocked that he got out of the jeep, walked up to the intruders and asked them to put down their sticks; if they didn't do so, they would be immediately arrested for trespassing. The graziers responded by beating up Fateh so severely that they broke his arms and legs and fractured his skull. They would have killed him if his driver Sayed had not jumped on his fallen body to take some of the blows. Fateh was hospitalized for three months but returned undaunted to the battle he would fight and eventually win. Great sacrifices were needed to defend Padmini's territory and the park as a whole. Fortunately she was able to continue the process of raising her cubs and our encounters with her became even more startling.

We spent as much time as we could with her and her new litter. This litter had one male and two females and I did not realize then that one of these cubs would become an all-time favourite. I would end up calling her Noon because she was most active at midday.

The monsoon was around the corner. It is a time when the forest becomes lush and dense. It is also totally inaccessible as the roads turn into slush and water crashes down from the slopes and cliffs. But the entire forest is transformed by the rains, and it looks magical.

We would have to wait until the end of the year before we next met Padmini and her cubs. In November, Fateh and I were driving around the lakes. We had just passed Badhyaya tracking around on his bicycle. Everything appeared calm. We had stopped to listen to animal calls when we saw a frantic Badhyaya pedalling furiously towards us on his bike. He yelled, 'Go to the corner of Rajbagh...there is a tree full of crows and tigers are on a nilgai kill.' This was rare. A nilgai or blue bull seldom finds itself the victim of a tiger's attack. It is big and there are only a few in the forests of Ranthambhore. Fateh and I rushed off to find Padmini guarding a male nilgai carcass. A bunch of nearly twenty crows sat on a nearby tree and white-backed vultures circled above. Three of her cubs were lazing around the carcass. A chunk from the rear had been eaten. We watched one of the best days in our lives with tigers unfold.

Even today, after nearly forty years, this remains one of my favourite memories of Padmini and her cubs. Fateh and I did not take a break all day and by the end of it were surrounded by nine tigers at different distances from the carcass. It seemed as though half of Ranthambhore's tiger population was around us. I noted in my field diary that the carcass was too heavy for Padmini to move but she had nibbled at the rump. Two of her cubs, sitting behind her and waiting impatiently for their meal, stood up to approach the kill. As they approached her, Padmini smacked one of the cubs with her paw and he submissively rolled over on his back. The other one began eating from the rump. Padmini seemed to be saying, 'One at a time.' At 7.30 a.m., Padmini grabbed the nilgai by the neck and tried to drag it away but its foot got stuck in a fork at the base of a tree so she settled down and started eating. When she had finished, she managed to drag the carcass about 8 metres away. We drove in further but were suddenly confronted by Laxmi, the female cub from Padmini's first litter. Five tigers were now spread out in front of us with both Padmini and Laxmi sprawled closest to the carcass. There was much nuzzling between the tigress and her cubs and Padmini marked a tree, sniffed the bark and again pulled the carcass further. This area was easily accessible to the jeep and as she pulled we moved in closer. A few minutes later Padmini decided to walk down the slope to the lake to have a drink of water. This was an opportunity for Laxmi, who darted in and started to eat. Padmini spent more than twenty minutes cooling off in the water and then settled on the path below. It was past 11 a.m. As we headed back to the carcass we noticed that a tigress we had named Nick Ear—she had a small cut in her ear—had arrived for the feast and had sat down near Laxmi. At noon Padmini appeared and snarled at Laxmi forcing her to move off the carcass. She then dozed off but kept watch on the crows whose cawing would alert her to any threat. Everyone was sleeping in patches of shade around the carcass. By 2 p.m. we had six tigers in front of us. It was an unbelievable sight. But the excitement did not end there. About 45 metres away from us, another tigress appeared amidst much snarling and growling. Things were getting nasty. Stunned at the scene unfolding in front of us, Fateh and I looked at each other as if in a dream. At 3 p.m. a large male tiger appeared in the distance, who looked very much like Akbar from Padmini's litter of 1976. Behind him was another tiger. Our hearts were thumping by now and we looked at each other in disbelief. We had nine tigers surrounding us at differing distances. Hardly daring to breathe, our eyes moved from one tiger to another. Not one of them was eating—Padmini appeared to be in command of the group and the dining. It was similar to a pride of lions on a kill—they do not eat together but take it in turns. Padmini's control of the group prevented conflict and injury among the tigers. By 4.30 p.m., as the evening shadows lengthened, Padmini moved off towards the lakeside vocalizing softly. At 5.20 p.m. Fateh and I drove off after ten hours of uninterrupted, extraordinary observation. Returning to the site the next morning, we found only Padmini and her cubs, one of the cubs preoccupied with chewing off the carcass's ribcage. The rest of the tigers had gone. An hour later Padmini and her family disappeared over the rise of the hill, leaving the remnants of the carcass for the crows and vultures. This grande dame had revealed one of the great secrets of the tiger's life to us—kin links remain and tigers can be tolerant of each other when they meet. More than three decades after this encounter, I believe tigers recognize each other in their lifetime and are able to share kills and have enormous overlaps in their home ranges. Some tigers are less tolerant and do not share their food but their individualistic behaviour is a part of the way they live.

◆

Tigers are voracious eaters. In approximately thirty hours, 250 kilograms of nilgai had been consumed. The search for food is a driving force in a tiger's life. Tigers respond to the chatter of birds, animal sounds and even trace the movement of vultures in the sky. These are all clues that lead to the feast. Each tiger needs fifty deer-sized animals to eat in a year—one a week. So, in Ranthambhore, if you have a population of fifty tigers they will kill 2,500 deer in a year and there would have to be at least ten times this number for the park's deer population to be sustainable. After dispatching their prey tigers prefer to drag carcasses to a thicker patch of forest to feed in safety. They yank kills in short bursts, either straddling them or pulling them in reverse. Smaller animals are carried off the ground. In Myanmar a tiger is said to have dragged a 770 kilogram bull gaur that thirteen men were unable to move even a metre. That is real power and is unmatched in the natural world. Tigers can eat more than 30 kilograms in one sitting and this ability is facilitated by their sharp carnassial teeth slicing at the meat while the molars and premolars grip it. Tigers have thirty teeth but they cannot chew easily so they have to swallow lumps of meat whole. The incisors (small front teeth) are positioned in a straight line, enabling them to efficiently pluck feathers and clean meat off the bone. The sharp claws are extended for grip and leverage while they eat. When unsheathed the claws are a mind-boggling 11 centimetres long. Rough projections on the tongue also help to remove hair and particles of meat.

◆

As the 1980s unfolded Ranthambhore's tigers were coming into their own. Those seriously interested in tigers were making it a point to come to Ranthambhore to observe its tigers. The lure of tigers can do crazy things to humans, as I knew from some of my own reckless and risky endeavours. One morning while I was in Ranthambhore I was accompanied by a senior forest officer. He had great experience in managing tigers and considered himself a wildlife specialist. He saw some tigers at close quarters on his first day. On the second day, when he saw a tigress sleeping in an open clearing near Malik Talao, he handed his driver a camera and asked him to take a photograph of him with the tigress. Against his driver's advice, this experienced forest officer got out of his jeep and approached the supine tigress. When he was 20 feet away from her, she let loose a blood-curdling roar, charged at the officer snarling viciously and ended up one foot away from him before retreating. The driver dropped the camera without taking a shot. The officer fell to the ground in a near faint and the driver had to carry him to the jeep and then to the rest house.

As can be imagined, my trips to Ranthambhore became more and more frequent. It got to be so that even with my eyes shut I could tell the exact location of the train on the Delhi to Sawai Madhopur line just from the sounds of wheels on the rails. For me the place was perfection itself, and every aspect of it was a tonic for the senses. Basking in the warmth of a roaring fire on winter evenings under the enormous canopy of the banyan tree, sleeping outside on hot summer nights, being ready to jump into a jeep at the sound of an alarm call day or night, listening to ghazals while drinking whisky with Fateh as the sun set and enjoying freedom that was unattainable anywhere else—all this and more filled me with a deep sense of contentment. Some of my best moments were spent with forest guards eating bajra ki roti with garlic and chilli paste, which was the staple diet in the area. In the summer onions were used in every forest post as a remedy against heat and dehydration. At one point, a night lens or image intensifier had been donated to the park. The huge 3-foot-long lens set on a tripod enabled us to view the park's night life. Fateh and I would go out regularly and spend the night at Jarokha in the Kachida Valley watching tigers or leopards who were lured by live bait. We had the exceptional good fortune of watching Padmini and her cubs feeding all night, one at a time under her watchful eye. At dawn the tigers would leave—they were still shy and mostly nocturnal in those days. On one occasion, we had a splendid night watching a leopardess and her three sub-adult cubs.

This was a time when one could walk freely in the forest. There were no tourists and no rules that prevented you from walking where you wanted. Tigers were difficult to see and fresh pug marks sent a rush of adrenalin and an intense desire to see the animal. Early one morning in May, as the sun was rising, I saw the fresh pug marks of Padmini and her cubs; they went from Jhalra to Nalghati but just before Kawaldar they vanished from the road. I was with Laddu, the tracker. We knew Padmini had entered the Nalsatka Nullah, thick and inaccessible and difficult to negotiate, but we decided to park the jeep and track her on foot. The nullah was covered with thick undergrowth and you never knew what was around the corner. We walked for half an hour as the sun rose. It was hot and I was perspiring heavily. We had a bottle of water between us and a couple of onions that might help with the dehydration. An hour into the walk I was getting really tired and was about to give up, bearing in mind that we had to cover the same distance to return to the jeep. But Laddu said, 'Ten minutes more.' I reluctantly agreed and watched a white-breasted kingfisher near a pool of water waiting to dive. As we walked around a clump of bushes, out rushed a snarling Padmini. We froze in our tracks. Laddu grabbed my hand and said, 'Don't run.' For a few seconds everything came to a stop. Then, fortunately, the tigress quickly retraced her steps into the bushes. It was then that I noticed some crows on a tree—she was on a kill with her cubs and we had intruded. My legs were shaking as Laddu and I slowly retraced our steps. I could only relax an hour later when I reached the security of the jeep. But even to this day, that encounter is frozen in time.

◆

As soon as the human disturbance in the park decreased Padmini slowly became more diurnal. If her first litter was mostly observed at night the second one was more in the day. It was through her that I was initiated into the secret world of tigers. She gave us our most memorable encounters and our records of them helped rewrite the natural history of tigers. Our amazing encounter with nine tigers still remains one of the rarest in the world and established the possibilities of kin links among tigers that allow for the sharing of food.

Padmini's second litter split up soon after the monsoon of 1981 and during the next years sightings of her became more and more infrequent. In our presence she had raised seven tigers, four males and three females. It was this generation of tigers that lived in relative peace as the villages in the heart of Ranthambhore had been successfully resettled. I saw Padmini for the last time in late 1982 while she was busy eating a piglet. She was alone. I watched her for more than thirty minutes and noticed that one of her canines was half broken and another worn off. I did not know how long she would survive but she had done her job. I did not know then but this would be my last sighting of her...a tigress whom we always thought of as the queen mother of Ranthambhore.

◆

It was in Padmini's lifetime that I also had encounters
with the two sadhus who lived deep in the heart of the
forest. The first was Kachida Baba and he lived in a cave
on a rocky outcrop at Kachida. Heavily bearded with long
flowing hair he was a regular sight as I set out tracking
tigers. Most of the time he sat in silence, deep in meditation,
in a lovely area that overlooked several small pools of
water and little waterfalls that spilled down from rock into
the forest. On rare days when he 'talked' I would discuss
tigers with him and he would always tell me of tigers that
slunk within feet of him as he sat on the forest floor. He
also told me that, like him, I would spend most of my
life in Ranthambhore. Fateh was keen that I spend a few
days in the cave with him but I did not go. I preferred to
limit my interaction with the holy men to our occasional
conversations about tigers. But these conversations were
illuminating. Kachida Baba would tell me of young tigers
that he saw fishing in the pools of water especially when
they were drying out in the summer. They would sometimes
grab the fish in shallow water and at other times smash
their forepaws on the edges to catch them. The other sadhu
Kawaldar Baba lived 12 kilometres away, also in a cave up
an escarpment. Below him were the most gorgeous pools of
water and a gorge that was exquisite. He had also watched
tigers fishing in pools of water in the summer. It would be
about thirty years before I was able to see for myself this
unique predatory behaviour in the very gorge in which
Kawaldar Baba had witnessed it when one of Machli's cubs

ran off with a fish in his mouth in 2007.

The diet of the tiger always astounds me—from fish, frogs, turtles, grasshoppers to peacocks, partridges, storks, jungle cats, leopards, bears, hares, crocodiles, monitor lizards, pangolins, snakes, deer and antelope, porcupines and ratels, civets, mongooses, small elephants, rhinos, wild buffalo and gaur—the list is virtually all-encompassing. The cubs learn how to catch small prey first and slowly graduate to the big mammals. They are expert hunters but can on occasion die at the hands of elephants, rhinos, wild buffalo and even poisonous snakes. Given the incredible diversity of their prey, cubs have to learn how a wide variety of species behave in order to be successful when they hunt.

◆

I should end this profile of Padmini by stressing the fact that the days that I observed her were among the most exhilarating and challenging of my life. Searching for her each day was like finding a needle in a haystack. At the time tigers were shy and elusive. Over the years, Padmini grew a little easy in our presence but the task of tracking her and her cubs challenged all our skills. That said, the levels of joy we felt upon seeing a flash of a stripe or the tip of a ear or the flicking of a tail could not be matched. Every little clue was vital and every little glimpse a stupendous surprise, as very few records or photographs of wild tigers existed at the time. Thus, it was that each time we saw her it was an unbeatable thrill.

GENGHIS—THE MASTER PREDATOR

THE FIRST TIME I SAW HIM WAS LATE IN OCTOBER OF 1983 as he leisurely strolled the shores of Rajbagh Lake. I knew a new male had arrived. He was a big guy with great ruffs of hair on his cheeks and a huge belly. He walked with a swagger as if he had not a care in the world—he seemed to know that this area of the lakes was his kingdom. It is after the monsoon that new territories are taken over and the areas re-marked as the monsoon washes off the scent of tigers. The lake area of Ranthambhore is a network of three lakes—Padam Talao, the lotus lake, and Rajbagh, the garden of kings, are separated by 20 metres and Rajbagh and Malik Talao by about 200 metres. Malik is small compared to the other two and all three are surrounded by a 10-foot-high khas grass wall that provides camouflage for both predator and prey. As the winter sets in and water starts to dry up in the hills the sambar move downwards in search of greener pastures. Their very special addiction in Ranthambhore is the succulent water plant that overruns the edges of the shallow waters and the lotus flowers that carpet both Padam Talao and Rajbagh. The sambar enter the water to feed and you can see their ears or antlers on the surface as they swim or wade through, gorging themselves on these water plants. They rarely bother about the crocodiles so acute is their addiction. This activity reaches a feverish pitch by March at the onset of summer and this is also when the crocodiles warm up to action and attack. (These cold-blooded reptiles do little in the chill of winter except take in the sun.)

Large male tigers are difficult to see in this setting. Our

only glimpses in 1983 were of the Bakaula male—a large, handsome male with a much darker coat than most, who in the hot summer was to be found in the cool jamun pools of Bakaula, or of Broken Tooth, a very muscular male, who would in a couple of years lose half an upper canine probably while attacking a sambar, as he paced up and down the Kachida Valley. The Bakaula male was sometimes invisible in the jamun groves and I remember one evening waiting for him to emerge for two hours. Finally, in sheer desperation, I started mimicking the tiger's call. In minutes an enormous tiger head emerged from the bushes and the animal paced towards me looking at me disdainfully before walking away.

We seldom saw a big male by the lakes so our sightings of the Bakaula male took one and all by surprise. He was my favourite big male of the mid-1980s. His coat was deep and rich and his face big. The ruff around the cheeks was full. He was easily the most handsome male tiger I have seen. He was very even tempered. He loved the cool waters of the Bakaula area where he could frequently be found immersed in the water, cooling off on a hot summer's day.

In November 1983, after an early morning drive I was lazing around on the balcony of Jogi Mahal when suddenly from across the lake came a cacophony of alarm calls of sambar. I was stunned to see Genghis racing after a young sambar who splashed across the edge of the water. Tigers wade through water and this was an activity that the tigress we called Nick Ear enjoyed in her early years. But I had never seen a tiger chasing a deer in the water. Genghis didn't falter and charged in as sheets of water splashed skywards from the flight of the sambar and the tiger's pursuit of the deer. He missed, but what a spectacle he had created. An orchestra of alarms resounded over the lake as sambar competed with monkey and peacock and greylag geese took flight. Genghis paused, looked left and right, surveying the chaos he had created, and then retreated into the grass. What I had seen was so intense that it was like being witness to a theatrical extravaganza.

Little did I realize then that this would be a major feature of Genghis's strategy from 1983-84. During that time he seldom strayed far from the lakes. He had adapted his predatory activity after assessing all the factors that had created this haven for sambar in the water and chital grazing on the green shoots at the edges of the lakes. In all these decades this behaviour of a big male only engaging with the lakes has never been repeated. For nearly eight months he remained rooted to the lakes, an area of 5 square kilometres.

My first encounters with Genghis were in the chill of winter. I remember 15 January 1984 vividly. It was a very cold night and I had just left the warmth of the fire at Jogi Mahal to head for my sleeping bag. As I was about to enter my room the resounding roar of a tiger shattered the silence. It was so close that I was stunned. Barely 15 metres away a black shadow walked across Jogi Mahal roaring continuously. The sound continued for nearly half an hour as the tiger walked around Padam Talao. As the tiger's roar reverberated in my head, I realized that Genghis was asserting his presence across the lakes. His sounds could attract or repel conflict and were like territorial signals.

The next morning was very cold. My hands froze on the wheel of the jeep and I could barely feel them. The forest floor was covered with frost. I circled Padam Talao and saw the scarlet sun peeping out over the hills of Ranthambhore. Slowly the day grew warmer as the sun rose. I searched the edges of the second lake and stopped to listen for calls. The sun flooded the lakes and was a delight as it warmed the body. This is always a very special moment in a forest— from freezing temperatures the warmth of the day warms every pore in the body. Suddenly on the path in front was Genghis walking towards me. The unmistakable glow of the striped coat, the powerful, unhurried, silent walk. The power and beauty of the moment was spellbinding. He suddenly flushed out a wild boar with three piglets from the high grass. They went scampering off in different directions. Within seconds, Genghis had pounced on a piglet and squeezed the life out of it. The sow stopped in mid-flight but there was nothing she could do to help her baby. Genghis carried off the piglet into high grass. A covey of quail came rushing out and in the distance peafowl called in alarm.

While Genghis was feeding in the high grass on the remnants of the tiny piglet, I parked 100 yards away at the edge of the lake hoping he would come to the water's edge. I suddenly spotted the sow approaching the grass to check on her baby but Genghis darted out and she fled. It is astonishing to observe the plight of a mother at the loss of her young. I have witnessed this even with deer as they approach tigers who have killed their offspring. At about 2.30 p.m. a group of sambar appeared on the shore and started to move towards Genghis. He suddenly erupted from the grass in a headlong charge, scattering the panic-stricken deer. The sambar flashed past our parked jeep and only at the last second did the charging tiger brake to a halt in front of the jeep. Slamming his forepaws into the ground he veered away, snarling viciously at his unsuccessful attempt. Thirty-two years later every detail of that encounter is still etched on my brain. The pure power of the tiger inspires awe. Genghis was a massive male tiger weighing approximately 230 kilograms with a thick ruff of hair on his cheeks and eyes that bored through you like a drill. Totally fearless he was always on the move and very active even in the middle of the day. Aggression was a part of his very nature—if he did not like human behaviour in the jeep he would be quick to snarl and even race up to you roaring loudly. He was a great tail twitcher and much more aggressive than either Padmini or Noon.

In late February 1984, as the seasons changed, I woke up at dawn to the death cry of a sambar in Padam Talao. I could see that a crocodile had made a kill. I quickly drove down to the water for a better look. But someone else had beaten me to it. Genghis sat on his haunches staring fixedly at the crocodiles trying to yank on the carcass. After forty-five minutes, as the sun's rays lit up the lake, he entered the waters of Padam Talao wading through lotus flowers towards the carcass. As he approached he was snarling viciously and beating his paws in the water to fight off the crocodiles. He snatched the carcass away, and with a firm grip on its neck, swam back to shore with his prize.

I was astonished to say the least. I would never have dreamt that I would see such tiger-crocodile interactions in the waters of the lake. Through March, April and May of that year it was non-stop—Genghis either usurping kills from the crocodiles or attacking sambar in the water. I must have witnessed at least fourteen kills being made. Noon, who was the area's resident tigress, and Genghis's mate, must have been watching carefully for she would learn this art of water predation from the master. I began to watch Genghis's every move. Fateh teased me that I had become Genghis obsessed. He wasn't wrong. I felt I was in tune with Genghis as I had observed him so intensely. It got to be so that I was usually able to find him whenever I went looking for him. Genghis was a tough tiger and highly individualistic. He was happy to be observed at close quarters but never permitted anyone nearby whilst eating. This was his private moment and if you ventured close he would snarl viciously and mock charge the jeep. I experienced this once and it was enough. Visualize an enormous male tiger snarling at you from 2 feet away. After that I never went near him while he was eating.

Being charged is a terrifying experience. A year earlier a tigress we named Nasty was always charging jeeps without warning. You would hear the rustling of the grass and then a growl so vicious that your hair would stand up and suddenly a snarling tiger would be a few feet away from the jeep. My hands at that moment couldn't even reach the ignition. I remember an incident when the tracker Gaffar was cycling through the forest and suddenly encountered Nasty, who began to chase him. Luckily, we were in the vicinity so Gaffar pedalled furiously towards us and leapt into our jeep, abandoning his bicycle in the forest. I have been charged countless times and on many occasions without warning or when I was unable to manoeuvre my jeep properly. I remember an occasion when I was following Nasty, approximately 50 feet behind, when she suddenly turned around without warning and raced back to charge the jeep roaring viciously. Even though I hastily got into reverse gear

I was on a winding road and could do little to get away. So I just sat and watched her vent her ferocity within feet of the jeep. We would shout and beat our tripods on the bonnet in order to stop Nasty in her tracks. Once Badhyaya was leaning on his bicycle and faced her fury. He got away unhurt but she smashed the rear wheel. But she never ever touched a human. On another occasion I had two elderly ladies in the jeep with me and we were sitting peacefully at the edge of Rajbagh near a patch of high grass and I was holding forth about the calmness of Ranthambhore's tigers when I saw the grass moving to my right and a snarling roaring tigress appeared a few feet away from the jeep. I shouted at her loudly. She retreated but the ladies in the back were in a cold sweat and one of them could not control her bladder. They cursed and shouted at me and I rushed back to base. Never again would they travel with me. Why this viciousness is displayed by some tigers is a question I still have no answer for. At least with Genghis you knew he would charge if you intruded on his feeding space. But Nasty was just unpredictable even though as I have said she never touched a human. She disappeared when the monsoon arrived and I never saw her again. I suspect she may have had an unpleasant experience with a jeep that either chased her or went in too close.

◆

My days with Genghis fell into a pattern. One morning, at the end of February 1984, I was driving around Rajbagh Lake quietly watching an osprey circle the waters and swoop on the unsuspecting fish below. I marvelled at the eyesight and ability of this remarkable bird. From the far side and close to the entrance of Rajbagh Palace I heard the booming alarm calls of the sambar echo off the waters of the lake. Quickly swinging my jeep around, I sped to the palace gates. A few seconds after I arrived there Genghis walked majestically out of the gate in all his splendour. As he passed my jeep he snarled in annoyance. I followed as he turned into a large grassy patch. By now the langurs were cackling in alarm from the branches and the spotted deer were going mad with alarm calls, their shrill cries interspersed with the louder and deeper calls of the sambar. The peacocks joined in as the lord of the jungle walked about and marked several bushes and trees and sniffed the area around them. He then walked to the edge of the lake and lapped up some water, occasionally snarling at a crocodile. A red wattled lapwing flew up in alarm and then tried to dive-bomb him. Genghis took no notice of this but walked leisurely up the hill near the lake and vanished. The symphony of sounds continued. I knew exactly where he was headed. He was taking the shortcut to Sukhi Talai which is at the edge of the third lake, Malik Talao. I quickly drove to the spot where I expected him to emerge. Ten minutes went by and there were no calls to herald Genghis's presence. He would enter the third lake without being detected. Suddenly I saw him walking slowly towards me with a swagger. He came within metres of the jeep and snarled at me, annoyed that I was already positioned on his path. He carefully walked into the high grass that surrounded the lake. I moved to the far side so as to get a good view of the expanse of water. Genghis was invisible somewhere in the middle. A group of painted storks were busy fishing the waters of the lake. It was 10.30 a.m. and I decided to wait, knowing that by 3 p.m. the first sambar would enter to feast on the succulent water plants. I watched a crested serpent eagle fly by. It was nearly 2.45 p.m. when a group of four sambar moved slowly towards the water. One of them had its tail up. They were moderately alert and clearly had experienced the charge of tigers. From the other corner six more sambar walked in, with two fawns accompanying them. The sambar slowly waded into the water. The tension mounted. It took an hour for the sambar to reach the middle of the lake and a few splashed near the shore where the high grass shrouded Genghis. Minutes later I saw his face peeping out and assessing the deer. Within seconds he ducked and I knew he was moving through the grass to the edge. Then like a bullet he raced out towards one of the fawns. Complete panic ensued as storks flew skywards and the deer tried to flee. Genghis chased first to the left but missed a strike and then swerved to the right but it was too late. The sambar managed to escape. Genghis stood in the water now deserted of life. One of the sambar called out in alarm. Genghis looked all around, slowly walked out of the water and wet and dripping re-entered the grass. It would take another couple of hours for the next group of sambar to appear. Nothing happened until dusk and it was time for me to head home.

◆

The seasons have changed by early March. The cold winter months are at an end and the onset of summer is just around the corner. It is early spring. This is a time when water dries up in the higher regions of the forest. The deer, especially the sambar, have moved down from the hills and to the region of the lakes both for water and for the succulent water plants. Sambar and chital congregate around the lakes and the sambar move into the water to feed on lotus leaves and other weeds. The lakes throb with activity. Genghis had by now sniffed out every inch of the lakes and must have realized the opportunities for hunting. By early March, Genghis was a regular feature there and on many occasions we found him camouflaged in the high grass that surrounded the lake. On one such occasion a sounder of wild boar unsuspectingly approached him and in a flash he pounced on a piglet and then swatted another with his paws. He then proceeded to carry them one at a time into a patch of grass to eat. We found him the next morning protecting the scraps of meat left from his feast. As I got closer he charged the jeep, coming within a distance of a few feet, and was completely aggressive and intolerant of any human around his kills. I should have realized that he still had remnants of his kills. I kept my distance. Even a mock charge is earth-shattering. After eating every bit of the kills he moved away from Padam Talao to Rajbagh where he went to sleep in the grass. He rested for the day in the grass and the next morning I found him in the high grass at Malik Talao peering out to see if the deer were within striking distance. I settled down to watch.

At 11.30 a.m. a group of four adult sambar approached him along the lakeshore. The high grass was ideal cover and the gap between grass and water was not too wide. As the sambar stepped into the water Genghis popped his head out of the grass and started moving diagonally through it in the direction of the deer. Just as he reached the edge of cover a peahen flew off squawking in alarm. The game was up. One of the deer turned, startled by the sound, and spotted the tiger. As it started to stamp its feet and bellow an alarm call Genghis charged but the bird had ruined his attack. The range was too great and the sambar leapt away to safety. Genghis stopped, looked around him in annoyance, and padded back to sleep in the grass. Despite the summer heat the lake was quiet for much of the day. A small herd of chital grazed on the far side of the lake; a few sambar entered the water but then drifted away. There was little activity in the tiger's vicinity. A couple of painted storks waded through the water and a sarus crane walked along the far edge. I had almost given up hope of the sambar returning. They seemed to sense the presence of danger. But then just after 5 p.m. two groups of sambar approached and from opposite ends moved towards the centre. There was a slight movement in the grass and I knew that Genghis had moved into a stalking position. Inch by inch I could see him move up to the edge of the grass unnoticed. He then peered out and watched what the sambar were doing with intense concentration. He stood for several minutes motionless like a statue. The next thirty minutes were some of the most tense and exciting I have ever lived through. I waited, gripping the camera with sweaty hands, and my heart pounding away. Genghis waited, frozen, as the sambar grazed peacefully in the water. He was measuring the distance and focusing on younger animals. Suddenly he exploded into motion. He entered the water with a great burst of speed. There was complete panic among the deer as the lake erupted in a profusion of spray. He bounded through, now after a young animal that had got separated from its mother and appeared to be doomed. He crashed into the terrified fawn at top speed bringing it down into the water. For a moment the tiger and his quarry were underwater and then with a huge heave he surfaced with the sambar. I watched in amazement a sight that in later years would rewrite the natural history of tigers. I had never ever read an account of such attacks in water. Genghis slowly moved out carrying his victim into the high grass. The sambar mother watched until the last instant. Peafowl flew all over the lake in disarray. I left in a state of elation. I had been privileged to witness the astonishing feat of a tiger successfully hunting in water. Even better, I had recorded it.

In April 1984, Genghis courted and mated with the resident tigress of the lakes, Noon. At the same time that she mated with him Noon also courted Broken Tooth who overlapped Genghis's territory around the lakes. But Noon did not conceive from this bout of mating. On subsequent occasions when she mated with both tigers it was impossible to tell which father sired the cubs. Genghis continued to hunt in the water into the month of May where his focus became Rajbagh, the second lake. Here he sought the thick cover of lotus flowers for his stalking of sambar. I had to look hard to find him among the pink and white flowers. He had his own eating spots around the lakes and one large bush was his favourite and full of the bones of past feasts. From the end of April to the end of May he spent twenty-four days on Padam Talao. It was very unusual for a big male to get rooted to a spot. They normally cover their large home range in the forest. Genghis had obviously decided that the lakes were ideal hunting grounds and therefore moved from one to another. Since early March we had seen more than a dozen natural kills. Given the high level of predation on sambar in the water I would often wonder why these deer kept returning—the only reason I could advance was the intense heat and their addiction to the juicy and succulent water plants. This became a fatal combination and still is today.

◆

There are an estimated 3,000 to 3,500 tigers living in the wild today. Tigers are very versatile animals, living in temperatures that range from -33 °C in the northern extreme of their range to 50 °C in the southern parts, and altitudes ranging from sea level to more than 3,000 metres. Not only do temperature and altitude vary greatly, so, of course, does vegetation, from the tropical forests of southern Asia to the coniferous and birch woodlands of Siberia. Tigers also thrive in mangrove swamps, dry thorn forests and tall grass jungles. They need only dense vegetative cover, sufficient large ungulate prey and access to water to survive.

The tiger's attack mechanisms are remarkable. The long leg bones above the knee joints provide leverage for handling heavy prey, while the extraordinary skeletal structure permits flexing, turning, twisting and the rapid grasping of prey using the heavily muscled shoulders and forelimbs. Tigers can, in short bursts, reach speeds of 95 kilometres an hour and jump up to heights of 10 to 12 feet. This flexibility is particularly useful when dealing with larger prey—a tiger learns from experience to avoid hooves, horns, antlers, even tusks, if its intended victim is a wild boar. The thirty teeth are vital for killing and eating. The two upper canines can be 5 to 7.5 centimetres long, the lower 2 to 5 centimetres long; combined with strong jaw muscles, they can deliver a lethal bite. The canines are rich in pressure-sensitive nerves, enabling the tiger to hit the gaps between the bones of the neck, biting into and sometimes rupturing the spinal cord. With heavier prey, the aim is to force it down and then strangle it, basically crushing the windpipe. Smaller prey can be dispatched with a single bite to the nape, which ruptures the neck vertebrae.

Stalking is a vital part of the tiger's hunting technique—the short lower limbs do not permit fast running, so the predator needs to be as close as possible to its prey before it is detected. In low light the tiger's eyes can detect any movement, as they concentrate available light on the retina, and the curve of the cornea creates wide-angle vision. Tigers also have binocular and three-dimensional vision and require only one-sixth of the light human eyes need in order to see. Tigers' eyes have special features to see in the dark. Large lenses and pupils receive more light; especially sensitive cells absorb the light. The retina contains two different types of light-receptor cells, which connect via the optic nerve to the tiger's brain. These cells are known as rods and cones; rods are more responsive in low levels of light, while cones are sensitive to high levels of light and are used in colour vision. Tigers have traded in more cones and in return acquired more rods so they have increased night vision useful for hunting at the expense of colour vision. Their tapetum lucidum, a reflective retinal layer, causes their eyes to glow at night and increases their ability to see in the dark.

As a tiger stalks it moves a few metres with muscles rippling and bunched up. Highly sensitive whiskers—nearly 15 centimetres in length—circle the tiger's head and lead the way. Every time its whiskers touch an object, the tiger blinks in response and is thus alerted to what lies ahead. Additional whiskers, known as superciliary whiskers, are located above the eyes and may have a protective function. Cheek whiskers appear further back on the face and are less significant. The sensitive touch of the padded paws helps in making the approach totally silent—avoiding even a dry leaf. The claws are retracted and this protects their sharpness. The ligaments hold them in their protective skin sheath and no muscular effort is needed. Only when necessary other ligaments pull the claws out or straighten the toes. These curved claws help young tigers to climb trees head first but to come down they have to crawl backwards or jump off. This is why adult tigers prefer not to go up trees as their heavy weight makes this process cumbersome.

Tigers creep, stalk and walk on their toes. The tail of the tiger does a lot of twitching and is highly sensory. A metre or more long it gathers a lot of momentum when swung from side to side, helping the tiger balance when he swerves or attacks during a chase. It probably also plays a part in tiger communication. A relaxed tiger has a droopy tail; a tiger meeting a friend waves a raised tail slowly. Twitching tails can mean possible aggression. Even the hairs on the back of the forelegs are responsive to touch. In the forest as against the lake area it is very seldom that you see the moment of impact when a tiger pounces on its prey. More often, you hear the kill and then come upon the aftermath. So even human ears have to always be alert to jungle sounds. I call it interpreting the language of the forest.

With his long bursts of speed, Genghis used the water to his advantage. Unlike Genghis, most other tigers take up a position near water or long grass and try to remain undetected until prey comes along. It is a game of patience and success depends on the wisdom and experience of the tiger. Usually one in ten attacks can be successful.

The way a tiger's skull is structured makes it a perfect hunter. Evolution has created a structure that is superbly designed for the job. A short, round skull provides more power behind the jaws than can the kind of long skull found in herbivores such as sheep. The tiger's bony septum, which separates the cerebrum from the cerebellum, and which in humans and many other creatures consists of only a membrane, increases skull strength. The jaw bones do not allow side-to-side movement, making the bite stronger and firmer. The jaw muscles, which are attached to a special bony ridge at the top of the skull called the sagittal crest, react quickly and can clamp down with crushing force. Genghis had a big head—it was one of the reasons he was a supreme hunter.

Genghis was now making effective use of the area of the lakes and fully utilizing it as his hunting ground. Noon kept away but I was sure she was watching. Genghis was using the heat and the receding water to his advantage and surprising the sambar who seemed slower getting out of the water than the tiger getting in. Genghis was almost showing off. His grass camouflage was perfect and he spent most of his time from the second week of March to the second week of April using the same strategy at Malik Talao. He killed six young sambar in front of me during the early summer. By the end of April, as the water receded even more, the gap between grass and water widened and his element of surprise diminished.

Genghis soon gave up on Malik Talao and switched to Padam Talao. I followed and soon realized that the best vantage point to watch him was from Jogi Mahal, my forest home. Besides charging into the water to kill, Genghis also tried two other strategies. In the first he would see a group of sambar from the grass grazing in the water and he would come right out in the open to watch them, causing such panic that the sambar would bolt in alarm. Padam Talao is a large lake and at least 10 feet deep in the middle. The sambar would not cross it and would flee to either side. With enormous bursts of speed, Genghis would cut off these exits and bring down his victims as they fled across dry land. To do this he sometimes had to run nearly 150 metres, which at full pelt is an amazing feat for a tiger and invites comparison with the technique of the cheetah. His other technique was to wade in and then swim out to the sambar in the lake and with powerful strokes pursue them, hoping that in the chaos that resulted an animal would get separated that he could then overpower with ease.

He patrolled all the sides of the lake watching the entry and exit points of sambar. Sometimes, in the intense heat of the afternoon, when temperatures soar over 40 °C, he would stalk sambar 200 metres away and then race into the water after them. On the shore he often used the jeep as cover and on many occasions stalked around my jeep to get at the sambar. He was a master strategist. Each of his water kills involved dealing with the marsh crocodiles that infested the waters of all the lakes. But I never saw him lose a kill to the crocodiles. In fact, as I have mentioned earlier, he scavenged the kills of the crocodiles if he ever saw them. He always came back wet, exhausted but victorious. He disliked the crocodiles and whenever near water was perpetually snarling at them. If the crocodiles attacked a deer Genghis would quickly turn up to annex the kill. If they were feeding on a deer that had died of natural causes Genghis would chase them off. He had little time for them and believed that all food in his range belonged to him! At that time there must have been more than a hundred crocodiles in the waters of these three lakes so while killing in the water he was often forced to face off against the big crocodiles. He always got the better of them due to his pure aggression. I would have loved to have had a camera under the water to watch the struggle but it was clear that both these predators were in perpetual competition. As Padam Talao had more water than other lakes, it attracted greater numbers of both sambar and chital to the lake's edge. As the chital gathered on the shore to feed on green shoots Genghis would race out and attack them. By June the waters of the lake were drying up rapidly and we saw less and less of him. The gap between the grass and the water had widened considerably.

I did not know it then but one of my last and most memorable sightings of Genghis that season was also a first for me. And it was not on the lakes. He was sheltering in a large bush when in the distance I saw a sloth bear approaching. As the bear walked by, Genghis leapt out of the bush and attacked the bear, slapping him with his paws. The bear tried to retaliate, rearing on his hind legs, but he was no match and fled.

Genghis was the monarch of all he surveyed and never tolerated any competition. In over forty years of watching tigers I have never encountered one like him. It was like watching a tactical planner who had evolved an extraordinary way of hunting after assessing the lakes and all their nuances. I ended up believing that I shared a sort of special relationship with him and I kept my fingers crossed that this might continue over the years. But I was proved completely wrong.

The monsoon of 1984 struck early. It was the last week of June and the rain poured down. I knew that within weeks the forest would turn from a burnt yellow to a lush green as the dhok trees put forth new leaves. I watched the downpour for nearly four days. On the fifth day the sun sparkled out from an amazingly blue sky. I drove into the park. Ranthambhore was gleaming and shining as if someone had polished it. Nature's cleaning service had not just washed and cleansed the park but left sheets of water behind. Padam Talao—the lotus lake—was flowing dramatically into Jhalra village and then falling into the Nalghati Valley. Never-ending streams of water gurgled away. Padam Talao and Rajbagh had got permanently linked at Mori where a stream of gushing water rushed across. Malik Talao was one enormous sheet of water.

Soon after the first monsoon rains Ranthambhore was transformed into a very special place. The strip of land that connected to Rajbagh Palace was completely submerged. Now tigers would have to swim across to get in. It was at the corner of Rajbagh that I found a very wet Genghis. He lay on his side and bunches of frogs jumped on his body and face. What a sight! That monsoon the forest guards lost Genghis. He was no longer around the lakes. I am not sure where he went but the monsoon is a time that tigers roam far and wide and I suspect he left the confines of the park. I hoped he would come back but Genghis never returned. I searched desperately for him in October 1984 but in vain. I could not believe that this unique and exceptional animal had gone. I missed him sorely.

In those days I had never imagined that poaching was even a faint possibility. Yet now, when I think of all the poaching that took place in the 1990s and at the turn of the century, I am sure that Genghis was the victim of a gang of poachers in the monsoon of 1984. His overconfidence and fearlessness probably led to his demise. There is no other reason why such a prime male tiger, with astounding success in hunting, would have vanished from an area of prime prey density.

I will never forget Genghis. He left his mark in the annals of the natural history of tigers and to this day audiences across the world watch films that he starred in. He left behind his art of killing in water for Noon and all the other generations of tigers to follow. This is the Genghis legacy and his imprint lives on even today amongst the tigers of the lake.

NOON—THE DIURNAL EXPERT

THE FIRST GLIMPSE THE WORLD HAD OF THE DIURNAL habits of tigers began with Noon. She represented the new generation of tigers that had grown up without human disturbance. It had been a long and hard struggle for Fateh to bring Ranthambhore to this point. An enormous team effort by both the district administration and the forest department had resulted in what was rapidly becoming the astonishing success story of Ranthambhore and its wild tigers. And it was Noon who filled the 1980s with her presence. Noon did not have long, flowing lines, she looked squarer and bulkier. Many thought that she looked a little masculine. Deeper colours on her coat and piercing eyes made her a striking presence around the lakes. Compared to her mother Padmini, she was much more diurnal and forever alert, always looking for an opportunity to attack prey.

After the monsoon of 1982, one evening in October, I heard spotted deer alarms followed by the most vicious growling and snarling around Malik Talao. I rushed off to investigate and found a tiger sitting on its haunches, panting heavily. As I crossed a patch of grass, I encountered two tigresses. One was sitting with her paws hugging the carcass of a chital doe, while the other watched alertly, moving a few steps forward slowly. The first tigress emitted a low growl and then with a loud 'woof' charged at the second. Both rose briefly onto their hind feet, mock-boxing each other, but soon the second one rolled over on her back as if in submission. The second tigress eventually started crawling towards the kill. Her head was close to the carcass and near the neck of the first tigress. The latter snarled viciously at her but it had no effect. Amazingly they sat like this without eating for thirty minutes. The growling, coughing and snarling rose to a crescendo. I had never heard this variety of tiger vocalization before. It was aggression through sound, for at no time did the two animals attempt to injure each other. Soon afterwards, the first tigress relinquished her hold and sat on the rump of the carcass to start feeding. The second immediately went to the neck and did the same. The dominant one plucked out the tail of the carcass and spat it out. The two tigresses ate ferociously from either side of the carcass, the dominant animal keeping up a continuous low growl. As they ate their aggression manifested itself in great pulls from side to side, and after forty-five minutes the carcass appeared to be splitting in the middle, held together only by the skin. Eventually it broke in two, the rump left with the dominant tigress and the neck, forelegs and chest with the second. They both crunched on for another thirty minutes; intestines, rumen and skin were all rapidly consumed. Later that afternoon this frantic eating was rudely interrupted by yet another tigress who rose from a shady spot nearby and charged the two on the kill, both of whom fled leaving the remains to the newcomer who immediately started feeding. She seemed to be the one who had killed the chital and permitted the first two to feed before annexing the carcass.

For many moments I was spellbound by this extraordinary encounter. At least two of these young tigers appeared to be Padmini's second litter. From their mouths had emerged a medley of the most vicious growls anyone could ever imagine. The third animal was the tigress I would come to know as Noon.

◆

In the early 1980s, the lakes were visited occasionally by a tigress who had a small cut in her ear, whom we called Nick Ear. She was very comfortable during the day and enjoyed wading through the waters of the lake. In fact, she was the first to haunt the Rajbagh Palace and some of my first photographs of tigers juxtaposed with the ancient ruins of Ranthambhore feature her. One afternoon she waded and swam through the waters watched by a herd of sambar standing on an islet in the lake. The scene was enthralling as tiger, deer and palace merged into one frame. It was a period of time when every day there was something new to be seen and Nick Ear was taking it all in. I remember one morning vividly. At the edge of Rajbagh there was a gaggle of greylag geese basking in the sun. Around them a dozen painted storks were busily fishing. We were driving past the deserted lake palace when suddenly the forest sprang a surprise. A shadow lurked in the chhatri of the palace. No. We screeched to a halt, moved in closer and were wonderstruck to find a tiger fast asleep under the chhatri. This was the last place I would have thought of looking for a tiger. In fact, it was a place I sat in to watch animals and birds on the lake. I soon realized that it was Nick Ear. She watched us out of the corner of her eye as she continued to laze in that incredibly historic setting. A few hours drifted by. Two crocodiles basked at the edge of the lake below the chhatri. The forest was peaceful. I thought of times past when kings and queens must have sat under this chhatri and gazed across the lake with music playing in the background. But times had changed. It was now Nick Ear's palace!

Sadly, by the end of 1982, Noon had thrown Nick Ear out. Once in control of the pristine, prey-rich lake area, Noon became totally diurnal and enjoyed her walks in the middle of the day, which is how she got her moniker. In fact, on many occasions she would so surprise the lake inhabitants, who were not expecting her in the middle of the day, that in the confusion she would expertly catch a deer. One of my favourite encounters with Noon was in early 1983 while sitting on the balcony of Jogi Mahal. I was sipping a cup of coffee watching deer grazing at the edge of the lake and a pied kingfisher hovering above ready to dive. Way in the distance I could see an osprey fishing. It was so calm and serene that tigers were far from my mind. Just past 11 a.m., from a bank of bushes in front, a tiger shot out at full pelt and leapt on a stunned spotted deer bringing it down, choking it in seconds and then quickly dragging it back into the bushes. It was Noon and she had allowed me to see my first kill in the day. Four other spotted deer were so shocked that they raced into the waters of the lake in a desperate attempt to reach the far shore. Right in the middle all four deer were gobbled up by crocodiles. A tiger's attack had led to a crocodile feast. I was aghast. My coffee had spilt everywhere. Within minutes the lake was as calm and serene as before with the pied kingfisher hovering above. Thus began my extraordinary affair with Noon.

The area of the lakes in Ranthambhore is where Fateh and I have spent the best days of our lives and where his ashes have been sprinkled and where mine will go. This is where Noon gave us a feast of activity in the perfect setting for wild tigers. Photographs of Noon taken by Fateh and me have travelled to every corner of the world. As I have said earlier, until the early 1980s there were few pictures of tigers in the wild. Hardly any tourists visited Ranthambhore but Fateh was determined to make it the most important wildlife destination in the world. Noon was the tigress who facilitated that process.

From 1983 the following decade was Noon's and she engaged me like no other tiger had done. I lived in Jogi Mahal, which was the heart of Noon's area, and in minutes I could rush off to find her.

Towards the end of May in the mid-1980s I received a cable from Fateh that read 'Come immediately. Noon has given birth to two cubs.' I was ecstatic. Noon was then five years old. I was in Ranthambhore by early June and Fateh told me how he had discovered Noon's very first litter a few days earlier. He had been in the middle of breakfast at Jogi Mahal when Badhyaya came running to tell him that road workers some 500 metres away had stumbled onto two tiny cat-like creatures in thick bush. Fateh had never seen newly born cubs but were they tiger or leopard?

Camera in hand he rushed off on foot with Badhyaya. It was dangerous but he could not take the jeep into the ravine. A tigress with tiny cubs will charge as aggression is a way to protect and defend cubs. Fateh had seen Noon mating twice so this bush required investigation. The tension mounted as they walked into a dense ravine. The fort of Ranthambhore loomed overhead. The road workers who had discovered the cubs stood by in a nervous cluster and Fateh told them to go home. Fateh and Badhyaya walked towards the thick bush in which the cubs had been found.

Fateh was not easily frightened by anything but he confessed to me that this was the most nerve-racking moment of his life—not knowing what would come charging out at him. He assumed the mother was away. Paradise flycatchers flew overhead. A couple of golden orioles flitted around a mango tree. A small stream flowed through the thickly forested ravine. The setting was wild and picturesque. The thick bush had a few bamboo plants around it and was dark inside. Gradually Fateh's and Badhyaya's eyes adjusted to the dark. Fateh peered in. A slight movement caught his eye as a tiny snarling striped ball revealed itself. Tiger cubs. Fateh quickly took a few photographs of what appeared to be two-week-old cubs whose eyes were open. In the distance peacocks started alarm calling. Fateh's heart thudded. Noon could be returning. He still had to confirm the tigress's identity, so he quickly told Badhyaya to close the tracks to all humans and then crawled up a ledge to a vantage point above the ravine. Two hours later he saw Noon approach the bush. This is what we had all been hoping for. She had a perfect den but it was too close to the road on which a continuous stream of pilgrims made their way up to the Ganesh temple each day.

That night Fateh was fast asleep on his roof under the open sky. In the heat of the summer sleeping on the roof is the only way to remain cool. At 4.45 a.m. the peace and stillness of the night were suddenly shattered by the alarm calls of sambar and the barking of a troop of langurs. Fateh, jolted from sleep, tumbled out of bed and looked down. A predator was on the move. The first rays of morning light crept across the horizon. On the vehicle track below Noon was striding along, carrying one of her tiny cubs in her mouth. She crossed some ruins and clambered over an ancient wall disappearing into one of the most inaccessible areas below the ramparts of the fort. She was changing dens and soon returned and carried her second cub to the new spot. Fateh watched from his roof. Noon had now found one of the safest spots in her range to den her cubs. This was a great relief for Fateh as she was now away from all human disturbance. For me it was the beginning of two splendid years of watching mother and cubs.

◆

Birthing amongst tigers is no easy process. After a gestation period of 93 to 110 days, the tigress chooses a safe spot to deliver her cubs. Cubs can be born within one hour but sometimes the birth can take as long as twenty-four hours, during which time the tigress gets some nourishment from eating placentas and embryonic sacs. The cubs are born blind and helpless, weighing between 0.79 to 1.5 kilograms. It takes anywhere from three to fourteen days for their eyes to open, though full vision is not acquired until some weeks later. There may be six or seven cubs in a litter though in Ranthambhore the average is three. The ratio of sexes at birth is one to one.

Early one morning on the day I was to leave a huge storm came crashing through the park—thunder, lightning and torrents of rain. Visibility was down to less than a metre. The monsoon was approaching. Within an hour the ferocious storm cleared up leaving in its wake a blue sky and the early morning sun. The forest was washed clean. The quality of light so special. The fragrance in the air magical. The leaves dripped with water and torrents of water cascaded down the hillside and waterfalls sprouted from the steep cliff faces and the edges of the fort. As we turned a bend in the road Noon crossed our path. One season had ended and another was about to start.

I was hoping that Noon's tiny cubs would engage us over the next two years like never before. And they did. This was the start of some incredible and magical years around Ranthambhore's lakes. Multiple tigers roamed the area. Noon had imparted her diurnal nature to her cubs so my encounters with them were now frequent. My most precious was in early 1985. I was breakfasting on scrambled eggs with Goverdhan, Fateh's son. It was about 11 a.m. when a sambar call made us jump. I said to Goverdhan, 'Let's go and check it out.' As we reached that magical area between the lakes I saw Noon moving with her cubs towards Mori. We followed slowly and watched her vanish into a thick bush. It was time for the tigers to rest—or so I thought. I turned the jeep to go back when a huge sambar stag came pelting out of the bush followed by Noon at full gallop. I followed quickly and there, right in front of us, on the jeep track, stood the stag and the tiger as if frozen in time. Noon had sunk her canines into the stag's shoulder but it was not a killing grip. They stared each other in the eye. Goverdhan woke me from my reverie, shouting, 'Start taking pictures. You will never see this again.' As we had left in great haste I had picked up the nearest camera but with no extra roll of film. The camera had only twenty-four shots left. I had to make every frame count. In front of me was everyone's tiger dream. In a clearing a tiger and a sambar face to face and frozen to the spot. All because Noon had got the wrong grip. If she had got the throat the sambar would have been down before I reached the spot. For eight long minutes they remained frozen and then suddenly the tiger changed her grip and attacked the sambar's hind legs and belly in an effort to force it down. Amidst much biting and clawing the sambar flopped down with Noon gripping its rear. Still no good for her. She had to find the throat but she could not release the grip she had. One of her cubs poked his head out of the bush as if expecting the feast of a lifetime. But in vain. After twelve minutes of struggle the sambar heaved himself up and kicked out forcing Noon to release her grip. The stag fled into the waters of Rajbagh. It was bloody and limping. Noon followed but was too exhausted and didn't give chase. Her cubs came around as if to egg her on but she snarled at them in irritation. The cubs ran ahead of her, following the sambar to the water's edge. The stag called out in alarm for the first time, a strange, dull and hollow sound as if his vocal cords had been damaged in the attack and waded deeper into the waters of the lake. Noon watched for a while from the shore. She was bleeding around the mouth—a bad kick. She slowly walked to the bushes where her cubs lay. The stag limped towards the far shore and stood motionless for many minutes in the shallow water. He then slowly hobbled out of the water and into a bank of high grass. His right foreleg looked twisted and broken. Many patches of his skin had been raked and he had a bloody swelling on the side of his neck. Goverdhan and I regaled Fateh with our encounter. He didn't believe us initially but slowly absorbed our euphoric state. Even today, more than thirty years after that incident, it remains the most important tiger day of my life. Noon had taught me an unforgettable lesson about the struggles of predation—the fine art so necessary for survival. I left the next day for Mumbai taking my precious camera roll to a special film processor. It took forty-eight nerve-racking hours to get the results and they were spectacular.

◆

Noon was a great scavenger of dead carcasses and would watch the skies for vultures. She would follow them to the feast, chasing them away on arrival. As a lake predator she was forced to interact with the crocodiles who would attack or scavenge anything near the shores of the lake. Crocodiles have a tough time tearing up a carcass and can take hours over it. Noon would watch and choose her moment perfectly to steal the carcass from them. On one occasion a large chital stag died of natural causes on the shore of the lake and attracted both Egyptian and white-backed vultures to it. A few king vultures hovered above. The vultures fought for supremacy and one of them, with wings flapping, stood on the carcass doing a typical goose dance thereby asserting its dominance. They then went for the meat. But this was not easy. The carcass was intact and without an opening. Amidst their jostling, flapping and fighting, the alarm calls of the sambar suddenly rang out. A huge crocodile was walking across the dry land towards the carcass. The vultures beat a hasty retreat. The crocodile clamped his jaws on the rump of the carcass. He tried to chew it but then realizing that his leverage was better in water dragged it to the edge of the lake. Several other crocodiles watched from the water, waiting to feast. It was dusk and we had to leave but the next morning Noon had successfully usurped the carcass from the crocodiles and was busy eating it in a bush.

Noon's exploits were slowly becoming famous across India and around the world. Tourism to the area was just starting and all those interested in wildlife wanted to come and see her. As I've said earlier, I lived then in Jogi Mahal in the very heart of Noon's range. I remember one night, late in March 1985, when I was enjoying my solitude staring into the embers of a small fire and chatting with Ramesh, the forest guard. Even today, when I sit by a fire, be it in India or Africa, it transports me to my memories of jungles and tigers. That evening, as I left the warmth of the fire, and got ready to sleep on the balcony of Jogi Mahal overlooking the lake, I could see the sliver of a new moon in the sky and the dark night glittered with a million stars that seemed so bright and so close that you felt you could touch them. The croaking of frogs and the chirping of crickets filled the stillness. Suddenly, from the spot under the banyan tree that I had just left came a tiger's roar, 'Aaoooo'. I knew it was Noon. The fort walls echoed with the tiger's roar and she moved from just behind me to the lake. For a tigerwallah the sound of the tiger is very special. That night I must have counted more than sixty roars that slowly faded away as she wound her way to Rajbagh and the second lake. Unlike other animals, whose vocal cords are triangular, the tiger's are square and allow the tissues to withstand more stretching using the pressure of the lower lung. It is this ability that creates such haunting sounds.

The next morning I got into my jeep and tracked Noon around the lakes. It is a delight to be up just before first light and in the chill of the morning. I could see the ramparts of the fort appearing and fading into the mist. A small gaggle of greylag geese flew across my path—probably ready to leave Ranthambhore for cooler climes. Peering out I noticed Noon's tracks as they left Padam Talao and crossed Mori into Rajbagh. I knew she would go to Malik Talao, and so I headed there. As I neared the lake, I saw a group of sambar and chital grazing in a grassy meadow behind the lake. I searched the edges of the grass with my binoculars. Partridges called endlessly but there were no signs of alarm amongst the deer. Suddenly, I saw Noon concealed in a patch of grass some 20 metres away. She was motionless, watching the movements of the deer carefully. Occasionally, a chital drifted a few metres closer to her and I could see her muscles ripple. At one point she rose on her haunches and peered carefully over the grass assessing her distance from the deer. She then quickly settled down and froze. Unaware of danger, a sambar moved some 5 metres closer to her. The tigress lifted her head, fully alert. Her tail twitched and a quiver ran through her body and then in a kind of slow motion she stalked forward with her belly touching the ground, much like a snake glides. The sambar was suddenly suspicious and stared in the general direction of the tigress but she was perfectly camouflaged. Noon dropped her head down. I could no longer see her. The seconds ticked by. The sambar was only 10 metres away but the tigress made no attempt to move. The sambar is a large, swift-footed animal and Noon knew she would have to get closer. A crested hawk eagle flew overhead. A couple of partridges scuttled away into a bush. A peacock cried in alarm some distance away. The sambar's tail was now up in suspicion and she slowly moved off. So did the chital. Noon watched but soon went to sleep. She rested in the grass most of the day hoping that another group of deer would come even closer. This is the endless game played between predator and prey, both trying to achieve their mission.

♦

In 1986, Prime Minister Rajiv Gandhi visited Ranthambhore with his family. News of Fateh's success with the tigers had reached his ears. Hosting the prime minister and his family was one of Fateh's greatest delights. And for a whole week Noon entertained the visitors, culminating in an attack on a sambar at the edge of Rajbagh. She raced into the shallow water missed one deer and killed another sambar in a flash as huge sheets of water rose into the air under the hooves of the fleeing herd. The time of her attack was just after noon and she dragged the carcass away to feed in high grass, only a few feet away from the prime minister. He wanted to see more of her and in high grass but his security personnel were reluctant. Eventually a bullet-proof vehicle was summoned and Fateh went into the high grass with the prime minister. They were stunned to see a big male feeding on the carcass. It was Broken Tooth. The prime minister was surprised to see Noon sitting and watching a little distance away. Fateh told me that the prime minister remarked that just like a traditional Indian woman the tigress had provided a meal for her mate! It was soon after this visit that tourism boomed. Another era was about to start. Fateh was thrilled. His dream of Ranthambhore being the ultimate tiger destination on earth was about to come true because of tigers like Noon.

A few months after the prime minister's visit, we were having a pre-dinner drink in Fateh's room on top of the entry gate at Jogi Mahal. Fateh called out to Ramesh to bring us our dinner from the kitchen at Jogi Mahal. A few minutes later I heard a rustling in the grass and peered over. There stood Noon, bathed in moonlight, with two of her cubs. She looked up at me. I hissed, 'Tigers' and we all went silent. We crept to the edge to watch. The tigers started moving down the path to Jogi Mahal. I saw Ramesh's torch as he carried our dinner to us from Jogi Mahal. Tigers and Ramesh were about to meet. Fateh shouted, 'Ramesh, go back…tigers.' Ramesh dropped the dinner on the forest floor and fled. The tigers walked on past the kitchen. Such encounters with tigers around Jogi Mahal became more and more frequent. We never knew when to expect a visit.

In Noon's first year as the resident tigress of the lakes, she engaged intensely with the big male whom we had named Genghis. He mated with her at the same time that Broken Tooth also mated with her. Her litter could have been fathered by either one of these big males. As we have seen, it was Genghis, the Lord of the Lakes, who taught Noon how to kill in the water. She attacked crocodiles, usurped their kills and chased sambar into the water successfully disposing of them Genghis style. After Genghis's departure Noon became his alter ego as far as killing in the water was concerned. In the first six months after Genghis left, Noon's water attacks were a little hesitant and lacked her mentor's expertise but slowly she mastered this art.

I remember one hot afternoon in March when Noon charged into the water from the grass, missing a sambar by inches. She then walked back into the grass and an hour later carefully watched another group of sambar entering the water some 100 metres away. In typical Genghis fashion she stalked the distance through the grass. She was developing her strategy through practice. She erupted from the grass and raced into the water a few feet away from the sambar but again the sambar escaped. I had now seen nearly twenty unsuccessful charges. Later the same evening, she charged yet another group of sambar in the far corner of the lake, this time chasing her victim across the shore to cut off its exit. But in vain.

At the critical moment of impact she would pause but she was learning from her mistakes. One day I watched her racing into the water after a group of sambar and in the confusion most of the deer fled but two helpless fawns remained and in panic moved into deeper water. Noon struck with lightning speed and killed one of them. I knew then she would be a real proponent of the Genghis technique. As spring and summer arrived her forays into the water became more regular, and in a five-week period between March and April 1985, Noon killed six sambar fawns in the water. The sambars' addiction to the succulent water plants continued, with complete disregard for the high level of predation they faced.

One of Noon's typical attacks to scavenge off the crocodiles revealed her mastery over this predator. Three large crocodiles had attacked a medium-sized sambar hind in the waters of Rajbagh. The depth of the water in which they struggled with the deer was not more than 1.5 metres. One crocodile made desperate efforts to yank off a hind leg, while another tried to grab the neck, amidst much turning and twisting of their bodies for leverage. The sambar was frozen, locked in by the jaws of crocodiles on all sides. Other sambar on the edges were calling out in alarm. After a few ear-splitting shrieks the captive sambar sank underwater and was hidden from view by a swirling mass of crocodiles. With much splashing and snapping the crocodiles tried to tear the carcass apart. It was a slow and noisy process. The reptiles didn't seem to have much success in feeding off the dead sambar. Suddenly Noon and her sub-adult cubs appeared, attracted by all the noise. Tigers will immediately respond to any sound of an animal being attacked either by other tigers, leopards or crocodiles. The cubs sat on their haunches as Noon circled the shore moving towards the crocodiles. She watched them for a few minutes and then slowly entered the shallow water. She gingerly picked her steps towards the action some 10 metres away. She paused 4 metres away and then with a burst of speed arrived at the carcass. She was smashing the water with her paws all the while and this forced the crocodiles to retreat. Twenty crocodiles glided away hastily. Grabbing the neck of the sambar, she pulled it through the water to her waiting cubs. A large interfering crocodile got slapped. After a Herculean effort she reached the shore where her cubs raced towards her. They nuzzled her and pawed the carcass but she still had to drag it 50 metres to the cover of high grass. While she was doing this her male cub pulled at her tail as if to say, 'I want to help.' Noon's male cub was slowly turning into a lake expert, following in his mother's footsteps. The female cub was reticent. The male was already charging deer on the edges of the lake. This was the same male cub who had once walked into the kitchen and lower balcony at Jogi Mahal and even sniffed at all the jeeps one night. Cubs are extremely curious and sniff out every detail of their surroundings.

By 1986 Noon was an expert lake predator and frequently clashed with the more than one hundred crocodiles that roamed the lakes. When the crocodiles found a carcass they had a difficult time tearing it apart as they had to wait until it putrefied in order to yank away chunks of rotting meat. Noon on her walks would detect this activity and then choose her moment to scavenge from the crocodiles. In the winter sometimes the crocodiles could take more than a day to rip open the carcass and then suddenly Noon would swing in to scavenge and feast on the reeking, putrefied mess. I once found a large sambar stag that had died on the shore of the lake. By evening Egyptian and white-backed vultures came to feed on the carcass. The vultures fought for supremacy and one of them, with wings flapping, stood on the untouched carcass. But the vultures were finding it difficult to tear the carcass apart. They needed a large opening for their beaks to hook into the flesh. Suddenly several alarm calls rang out as a large crocodile moved towards the carcass forcing the scavenging birds to take off. Just as with the chital carcass I have described earlier, Noon would steal this carcass. She appeared and began to watch the commotion. She must have followed the vultures in. The first crocodile tried to drag the carcass to the water but it was too heavy and he could not budge it. Several other crocodiles watched from a distance. It was the first time I had seen Noon watching crocodiles and deliberating on what to do. Unable to pull the carcass away, the crocodile eyed the tigress warily. They looked at each other as if assessing each other's abilities. At dusk Noon gathered up her courage and moved in with a roar, and the large crocodile fled. He was vulnerable to a tiger's attack on dry land and therefore only felt safe in the water. Noon gripped the carcass by the rump and dragged it into cover to feed on. Where in the world can you watch such encounters between tigers and crocodiles?

As I've mentioned earlier, Noon fraternized with two male tigers in the area of the lakes who were both very different from each other. When Genghis left in the monsoon of 1984 he was replaced later that year by Broken Tooth. Noon's regular predation in the waters of the lake meant that he could annex her kills. But I never saw Broken Tooth killing in the water. Tigers are very individualistic and develop their own temperaments just like human beings do. If Noon mimicked Genghis, Broken Tooth never mimicked Noon as far as water-based predation was concerned.

In the mid to late eighties, whenever I found a tiger, I would try and spend the day with it. Most of the time tigers laze about and sleep. This is how they conserve their energy. I remember seeing Noon sprawled out one morning at Malik Talao. Seven hours later she was still supine. I considered going back to my room to have a chilled beer and a nap but the tiger's lure proved much stronger. You never knew what could happen when you were in the presence of a tiger. I suddenly noticed a troop of langurs behind Noon jumping around on the branches of a ber tree as they fed on the fruit. Noon briefly raised her head to watch them and then went back to sleep. At 5 p.m. I noticed a langur climb down from a tree and start the long walk to the lake to quench his thirst. Noon was positioned strategically. The langur's approach would be within feet of her. Apart from a flicking ear, which told her about the rustling of the grass, she remained still, eyes closed and without movement. When the langur was 10 feet away and totally oblivious of the danger he faced, Noon sprang on the defenceless victim with a lightning–fast leap. For a split second the langur was stunned, paralysed by the sight of this leaping apparition. Noon seemed to pinion the monkey first with her forepaws and then took a grip on its rear flank with her canines and quickly shifted to its neck as the monkey shrieked and struggled. All this was taking place in fractions of a minute. It was the first and last time that I saw a langur kill—so rare amongst tigers.

◆

Young cubs learn about hunting from the age of three to four months and stalk anything that moves—insects, butterflies, frogs, partridges and even quails. In peacock-infested forests they chase and eat peacocks, plucking off their feathers and devouring their meat. I watched Noon and her sub-adults race after a single peafowl and swipe it with their huge paws before its clumsy take-off. Noon would also devour porcupines. She was never injured by a quill but I have seen other tigers embedded with quills that they try desperately to pluck out. It is astonishing how they enjoy feeding on an animal that is so tough to kill. Another animal that is occasionally killed is the ratel or honey badger, which sometimes arrives at carcasses to scavenge. The ratel is a very elusive creature and my only sighting of one was on a sambar kill that was being fed on by both crocodiles and jackals. The crocodiles had left the water to feed in the forest and a ratel watched the scene. I haven't seen a tiger attacking a ratel but I did once observe Noon carrying a dead jungle cat in her mouth that must have somehow got in her way. As I have mentioned earlier, the tiger's diet is very diverse and can include fish, turtles, snakes, crocodiles, monitor lizards and even grasshoppers. In Ranthambhore I once saw a young male tiger playing with a softshell turtle that he held between his paws and tried to devour.

Sometimes, when she was hunting, Noon would look skywards and follow the direction vultures took, especially when they were flying low and swooping to the ground. I once watched her following low-flying vultures at a fast trot from one lake to another until she found the carcass of a young sambar. At the time, Ranthambhore was full of white-backed vultures. Sadly today there are hardly any left. A chemical injected to treat livestock proved harmful when ingested by vultures scavenging on carcasses, resulting in their population being wiped out. India lost a cleaning service provided by nature. Noon lost her food finders. In the absence of vultures crows are good indicators of kills and the chatter of tree pies can also lead to a carcass. But when a tiger turns up, vultures and crows become the object of the master scavenger's wrath.

At the end of 1987, Noon had her second litter. In the first months after they were born, the cubs were very curious and playful. They centred their activities in the vicinity of Jogi Mahal where they were born. One day we followed them into one of their densest day shelters and found the male cub perched high up in a tree. Up to the age of fifteen months the cubs enjoy climbing and sitting on trees. They are light enough so the branches don't break. Noon sat below and watched as the female cub tried unsuccessfully to clamber up to her brother who kept smacking her down. Soon the cubs abandoned their game and snuggled up to their mother. As she licked both of them, they rubbed cheeks and flanks with her. One of the cubs jumped over her and caught her tail. She then rolled over on her back as one of the cubs stretched across her belly. The cubs chased each other around, leaping at each other, while standing up on their hind legs. Wrestling and gentle sparring strengthen the family bond and this use of their limbs is vital to develop their strength.

In late January 1988 we set off in search of Noon and her cubs on a bitingly cold morning. A langur was barking in alarm at the edge of Rajbagh and we went off to investigate. The sun was rising over the hill and as we switched off the engine we were greeted by a cacophony of sambar, chital and langur alarm calls. At one corner of the lake Noon was walking along nonchalantly with a chital fawn swinging from her mouth. A few peahens took flight. She headed for a bank of high grass. Suddenly two peacocks flew out of the grass followed by two racing cubs. They rushed to Noon and the male cub grabbed the fawn and darted back into the clump of grass. Noon licked the female cub and they both reclined at the edge of the grass. They waited patiently for the more aggressive male to have his fill. The male polished off the best parts but was soon pushed away by Noon amidst much growling. She picked up the remnants and her male cub moved away. The female cub joined her mother and they chewed on the bits and pieces that were left. After an hour mother and cubs left the grass and walked around the shore towards Padam Talao, the first lake. The cubs were in a great mood and jumped and chased each other as they walked. One charged into Noon and she snarled in annoyance. They now reached the edge of the first lake near the masjid; the cubs went along the side of the lake and Noon followed the jeep path. In between there was forest and deer. Suddenly two sambar alarms blasted out from the lake as the cubs flushed the deer. Noon was now completely alert and darted rapidly on to the track realizing that the sambar were in between her and her cubs. There was a thud of hooves as Noon settled down on her belly, completely still, at a point where the animal track joined the road. A large rock hid her. She had judged the exit perfectly and it looked as if her cubs were helping. Suddenly she leapt up and I saw the flash of a sambar head going down. A grunt and a dying croak were all we heard as she clutched the throat of a sambar hind. It was a perfect grip and the sambar's legs twitched in vain. The cubs approached the carcass but were frightened by the thrashing leg movements of the sambar. In minutes the sambar was dead. The male cub came in and rested his paw on the sambar's shoulder. I was astounded—two kills in less than two hours. The female cub sniffed at the carcass and soon Noon dragged it into the thicket. The cubs had watched the killing and helped to flush out the sambar. They would now feast for a few days. We had seen the first joint forays made by the mother and cubs—these would help the cubs develop and fine-tune their hunting skills.

◆

Tigers develop into highly individualistic animals. As you watch them over the years, their distinctiveness becomes immediately apparent just as with human beings. In 1988 Noon was nine years of age and weighed close to 180 kilograms. Her lower right canine was half broken. As we have seen, she could hunt at any time in the area around the lakes taking advantage of the diurnal behaviour of deer. She was a much more aggressive hunter than Laxmi, whom I will profile in detail later in the book, and, on open ground, favoured long bursts of speed to corner her prey. Laxmi would use much shorter distances, hiding in cover and stalking her prey.

Tigresses like Noon enjoyed preying on wild boar, especially piglets. Great care was taken while attacking adults. Tiger lore is full of stories of wild boar chasing tigers away. When I bought some land in the area in 1988 I saw such an encounter in an adjacent agricultural field. I was with Goverdhan when I heard the vicious growl of a tiger at 8 p.m. We approached the spot on foot and in the light of our torches we saw a tiger and a male boar face to face. The wild boar kept charging the tiger and the tiger kept dodging but finally gave up and vanished into a wheat field.

By the age of sixteen months the cubs have grown large. They wander around their mother's range keeping in touch with her through scent and sound. Noon tried her best to encourage their independence. I remember late one evening around Malik Talao a burst of alarm calls indicated the presence of Noon in a clump of grass. As we approached she charged and killed a chital fawn. As she walked along, carrying the dead fawn, her cubs darted towards her. The male attempted to snatch away the fawn. The cubs were now large enough to battle for the fawn; the female gripped one end of it and for a while both cubs remained motionless holding onto either end of the fawn. Then began a frantic tug of war and the fawn was rocked from side to side. This time around Noon reclined to one side as her cubs fought over the right to eat first. Several shattering growls later the male cub had won the bout. It is at this age that the cubs are forced to fend for themselves and make their first attempts at stalking and hunting peafowl, monkeys and fawns. It is a critical period where their ability to survive is tested. Noon's absences from her growing cubs became longer.

Noon had to be very careful about other male tigers who could intrude into her territory. For example, Broken Tooth, whom she later mated with, encountered her over one of her kills. She boxed him on the nose to defend herself. She lost the bout but fortunately didn't suffer much damage. Such fights can be vicious and I know of at least one case in which a tigress killed a tiger, in order to protect her cubs. The male cub faces the biggest threat from transient male tigers.

Our final observation of Noon's second litter was in May 1989. Late one afternoon we were watching large herds of chital congregating on the shores of Rajbagh Lake where the waters were fast receding. It was hot and in a month the monsoon clouds would fill the sky. Suddenly the male cub moved out of a patch of grass watched by hundreds of chital, all alarm calling in panic. But he was in no mood to hunt. Looking well fed he walked leisurely to the water and settled in it to cool off and quench his thirst. The deer alarms petered out. Half an hour later Noon appeared on the far side and did much the same thing and then 30 metres away the female cub came out to cool off. The cubs were now nearly their mother's size. The three tigers soaked in the water. The deer watched but continued grazing. The sun was setting. It was my last day in Ranthambhore on that visit. The saga of this family group was nearly over. I wondered what the effect of the monsoons on the family and other wildlife would be. Would the crocodiles survive? Would the family split? Would I find the three tigers together after the monsoon? When I returned a few months later they had split up, meeting only occasionally.

Noon survived the 1980s and my last sighting of her was in the summer of 1990. I will never forget that encounter. She walked slowly to the edge of Rajbagh Lake. She looked older. Tigers change colour as they age especially around the face where the hair grows paler. The monsoon would soon crash down and I was not sure if I would see her again. The sun was setting and the light glanced off her back enveloping her in a golden light. I was alone in the jeep and this vision of her seems as if it happened yesterday. By this time she had successfully raised her second litter and in her last years had delighted the world with her water kills, racing into the shallows of the lakes, causing chaos amongst the grazing sambar, and more often than not bringing one down. The world's photographers and film-makers arrived to record this unique behaviour and she became famous around the world. The tourist boom followed. As Fateh had predicted, Ranthambhore had become the best place in the world to see wild tigers. There was no shortage of high profile visitors after the visit of Prime Minister Rajiv Gandhi—among them were John F. Kennedy Junior and Mick Jagger. Sawai Madhopur was no longer a one-horse town. Numerous taxi jeeps lined up for the visitor and open buses took larger numbers into the park. Hotels mushroomed along the road to the park and the Ranthambhore I knew slowly changed. I was sad as the tranquillity of the forest dwindled more and more. You had to go deep into the forest to find peace. But I couldn't really complain because tigresses like Noon had drawn the multitudes to the forests of Ranthambhore and transformed the local economy. Most of the 250,000 people living in the area benefitted from the boom. They owed their improving prospects to Noon.

As for me, she was a tigress who filled up my senses. I grew really close to her and missed her when I could not find her. Indeed, she grew to be a most pleasant obsession of mine in the 1980s. I am reminded here of a comment Fateh had teased me with—that I had fallen in love with a tigress. I know that whenever I arrived in her presence there was a quick look of recognition and then most of the time it was just her and me. Many scientist friends warned me to keep detached and not humanize tigers but in truth I was delighted with my emotional engagement with Noon. It deepened my understanding of the secret life of tigers. I do not think I ever experienced such closeness with a tiger ever again. Some of this had to do with the fact that it was a time when I could drive out on my own and watch tigers in solitude. There were fewer rules and less demands by visitors—this helped in building my amazing relationship with Noon. She is gone but endures in my heart and my mind. Even today, when I traverse the lakes, which were at the heart of her territory, I can summon up images of her slicing through the waters of the lake or erupting from a bank of grass in her incredible pursuits of deer. Images that will always remain etched on my mind.

Noon and her pattern of behaviour and use of the area were imprinted on every subsequent lake tigress that ruled over this space. Even after more than twenty years every resident tigress of the lakes still uses the same paths and walkways, and day shelters. There are individual variations of course but the patterns are startlingly similar. That in itself is a remarkable revelation.

BROKEN TOOTH—THE GENTLE MALE

THE ENTIRE 1980S WERE THE YEARS THAT BROKEN tooth—or Kublai, as Fateh preferred to call him—ruled the territory that I traversed. He patrolled the Kachida Valley and the edge of Lakarda where the Bakaula male reigned. He made the rounds of the lakes and the Nalghati Valley, traversing more than 100 square kilometres. During his reign he expanded his domain considerably while in his prime but his field of influence decreased towards the end of the 1980s. Broken Tooth vanished after the age of twelve but in those years we had an ongoing photographic record of him.

I first photographed him one night when he was eighteen months old, just when he was about to separate from his family. For male tigers this is the beginning of a challenging period. By twenty to twenty-two months they lose all contact with the mother and move to the fringes of an area to hunt, eat and develop in size, strength and ability. It takes a year and sometimes even two years for them to mature to match the powers of the resident male. Sometimes they can be pushed out of the park. A few have been known to move from Ranthambhore all the way to Madhya Pradesh. Tigers are very difficult to see or find during this period after dispersal from the family unit. By paying attention to the scent marks of other tigers they stay away from any direct confrontation. If they encounter a big male the conflict is usually soon resolved. I once witnessed such an encounter between two males late at night. One was slightly larger than the other. They rushed at each other with the most blood-curdling roars. It was chilling to watch. Nose to nose they snarled ferociously at each other but in seconds the younger male dropped to the ground and rolled over on his back in a gesture of submission. The conflict was over and the resident male silently walked away. Serious problems arise when males of equal strength compete with each other and neither is ready to submit. In some of these encounters a tiger can be killed and eaten by the victor. I have never encountered such an event but there are many records of fatal encounters from across India. There are times when a tigress can confront large transient males. As I've said in the last chapter, I know of a case where a tigress confronted and killed a big male to protect her cubs. She even opened the carcass of the male and ate a bit of the rump. Roaring loudly, she then took her cubs away.

I do not know what tortuous experiences Broken Tooth went through between the age of two and four years but he survived and took over a prime bit of tiger turf. He was a gentle male who was rarely aggressive in my presence. He kept his distance from human observers unlike Genghis and if you got too close he would tend to move off. He was squat-bodied and when full of food the folds of his belly nearly scraped the ground as he walked. He was much paler then Genghis and less adventurous. A few years after I saw him he broke half a tooth probably while killing a sambar and assumed his name. Earlier we had referred to him as the big male of the lakes.

During his first five years he remained elusive. In 1983-84 he kept away from the lakes because Genghis ruled. But even so he found a way to keep in contact with Noon. When Noon was ready to mate she found a way to mate with both Genghis and Broken Tooth. He spent more time with another tigress called Nalghati who lived in the Nalghati Valley, the area adjacent to the lakes.

It was with Broken Tooth that I saw my first and last camel kill. A stray camel had found its way into the Kachida Valley and the next morning it was dead, killed by this powerful male. The tiger must have leapt at the neck and forced the huge animal down before throttling it. Broken Tooth spent six days feeding on his victim, finally leaving the leftovers to the winged scavengers. He was the only tiger who attacked big wild boars. Tigers prefer to keep away from wild boars which can be aggressive and are able to charge tigers and cause injury with their small tusks. Broken Tooth would effectively bring them down and feast on them. I have seen at least five wild boar kills on the edges of Malik Talao that he devoured.

Big males like Broken Tooth enjoy walking. I remember a day in the early 1980s when I saw Broken Tooth in the middle of the road as I entered the gate at Jogi Mahal. It was 7 a.m. and I followed him as he skirted Padam Talao. When the resident male arrives in an area he usually leaves territorial signals by marking all the trees. That morning Broken Tooth was in a marking mood and he must have spray-marked three trees before he sniffed the air and hung his tongue out in a display of flehmen, the tiger's behavioural response to another tiger's scent. In this gesture the tiger curls back its upper lip exposing its front teeth and inhaling heavily. This position is held for several seconds and facilitates the transfer of pheromones and other scents into the vomero-nasal or Jacobson's organ located above the roof of the mouth via a duct behind the front teeth. These chemical cues provide enormous information on the reproductive status and freshness of the presence of tigers. The tiger scans the area and then re-marks the spot where he has identified another tiger's scent. This signal is important to attract or repel conflict.

Broken Tooth that morning was out to find Noon and walked to Mori and then around the lake. In about half an hour he marked sixteen bushes and trees. He then stopped and stretched his forepaws on one of the trees and for a moment it looked like he was giving the tree a bear hug. He raked his claws on the bark, leaving yet another signal of his presence before moving on. He soon left the second lake and moved to Malik Talao. Sambar and chital raised the alarm as he walked but he was unconcerned by the reception he was getting. As he approached Ghazal Hill he swerved off. In the distance some nilgai females were grazing with their young. They had not spotted him. Broken Tooth was now fully alert as he carefully paced towards them. There were enough bushes for cover. The nilgai continued to graze. With his powerful muscles rippling, Broken Tooth got into a stalk and glided forward in slow motion. Now the forest hid both predator and prey. For many minutes nothing happened. Then the strange alarm call—like a booming burp—of the nilgai resounded twice. I tried to reposition the jeep but the terrain was tough to negotiate. When I finally found a clearing I saw the most amazing spectacle. Broken Tooth was straddling a sub-adult nilgai. He turned around for a second to look at us and then gripped his fresh kill and started to drag it up the slope of a hill. As he vanished from sight, I thought it had been a special morning because it is difficult to spend long periods of time with big males. Females are easier to follow as they spend most of the day or night hunting, especially when they are with their cubs.

One of the most interesting aspects of the way how tigers hunt is that, unlike many other predators, they do not seem to single out the young, the old or the sick to prey upon. In fact, their preference is for larger, healthy prey.

◆

Walking with tigers is a great delight. Especially in the early morning. As the sun rises the golden light slides off the tiger's body. It is a magnificent spectacle. In the winter as the tiger breathes, puffs of mist explode from his mouth. Sometimes these walks lead him to the resident female and her cubs. He checks his harem and bonds with the cubs. Tigers can walk more than 10 kilometres in a night and Broken Tooth was no exception. As has been noted, males are territorial and as they walk they sniff their marking trees and spray them. They can do this every 100 yards especially after the monsoon as their scent gets washed out. I have described how Broken Tooth clawed at a tree. You can often find trees that are claw-marked by tigers. It probably reveals their size and embeds their scent in the bark. It could also be a visual signal. This reasserts their presence and can attract or deter conflict. If the scent is fresh, other tigers mostly change direction to avoid clashes. However, if a new male wants control of a territory he will follow the scent until he finds the resident. A battle royal could follow but I have never witnessed this between equally powerful males. In Ranthambhore conflicts were mainly resolved by scent marking. Scrape marks are also left behind on the grassy verges of paths and roads. Male tigers defecate at important spots in their range.

Tiger faeces or scat provide us human observers with information on their diet and what they consume but also the exact DNA of the animal. The scat is covered in a layer of cells from the intestinal wall. When defecating some of the epithelial cells that line the colon scrape off with the faecal matter. From this, the DNA can be extracted to identify individual tigers. Genes can reveal the secrets of eating habits, courtship, mating behaviour and genetic diversity. This non-invasive research is vital to the conservation of wild tigers.

◆

Observing Broken Tooth resulted in some exceptional encounters. I remember one early summer day when I found Nalghati and Broken Tooth under the shade of an exquisite flame of the forest tree. They sat 20 metres from each other amidst the red flowers that carpeted the floor. In typical tiger fashion they were conserving energy and sleeping. We thought that Nalghati had produced cubs but there was no sign of them. The next morning, in the same area, a pair of king vultures were perched high up on a tree. Scores of white-backed vultures filled the trees all around. A pair of Egyptian vultures circled low over a dense grove of bushes and shrub. Above one of these bushes flew a bunch of crows and we knew that a tiger had killed; the crows were circling the exact location of the carcass. Going cross-country we soon found Broken Tooth lazing under the shade of a tree. He looked stuffed and enormous and probably weighed 225 kilograms, after his huge meal. Nalghati was much further off, protecting the carcass of a sambar hind from the scavenging birds who were in a frenzy to feed. There were no signs of the cubs. A part of the rump of the sambar had been eaten. By the afternoon, when the temperature must have been 45 °C, both tigers looked hot and bothered. A hundred metres away was a small waterhole and we decided to sit there hoping both tigers would turn up to cool themselves from the blistering heat.

Shortly after 4 p.m. Broken Tooth ambled towards the pool, slid into the water hind legs first and soaked himself completely, leaving only his head visible. I have seen tigers doing this frequently and it appears that they do not like water splashing in their eyes and prefer to look outwards from the water, which enables them to watch out for approaching prey or other tigers. When they need to cool off tigers sometimes step into a pool of water face first and splash water in their face. But eight times out of ten they back into the water and look outwards with their face right on the edge of the water and the body inside the water to keep cool. About twenty minutes later, Nalghati followed and both tigers lazed around in the water. My camera clicked furiously. Suddenly Fateh said, 'Valu look.' We froze in delight. There in front of us was a male cub, four to five months old, nonchalantly walking towards the pool. Without fear, and as if he had done this before, he circled the adults and entered the water close to Broken Tooth. Within seconds a female cub followed and entered the water to sit near her mother's paws. The tranquillity of the scene was extraordinary. All four tigers cooled off.

For centuries the father was considered a threat to young cubs but what Fateh and I observed would rewrite the natural history of tigers. Nalghati licked her female cub.

They all quenched their thirst then the male cub rose and nuzzled Broken Tooth before leaving the water. The female cub followed and both cubs played and leapt at each other, slowly moving towards a tree on which they clambered up and down. A game of hide-and-seek ensued as they peeped at and stalked each other in the foliage while the parents watched. Soon Nalghati got out of the water and vanished into the forest. The cubs continued to play under the watchful eye of Broken Tooth. At dusk he slowly heaved himself out of the water and walked towards the cubs. They rushed up to him and nuzzled him. He licked one of them. They all then sat down a metre or so from each other. Fateh and I had witnessed one of the most closely guarded secrets of a tiger's life—the resident male interacting with one of his families. Fateh's photographs were some of the first ever taken of an entire tiger family—including the big male—all together.

◆

It was usual for aggressive big males like Broken Tooth to annex the kills of females forcing them to wait until they had had their fill. I remember an incident from the Kachida Valley where Noon had brought down an adult sambar hind. She had just started eating from the rear flank when Broken Tooth arrived and walked in with a swagger. He must have sniffed her out. His arrival was heralded by a roar and though Noon snarled back she was no match for this big male. She retreated submissively and sat 50 feet from the carcass. Broken Tooth feasted for most of the day. Big males can eat 30 kilograms of meat in one sitting and by the time he was finished with the carcass the best chunks were gone.

Noon only fed the next day. I recall another younger female hovering around in the area with a bloody gash in her flank. She must have tried to muscle in and was probably walloped by Broken Tooth. Encounters over food can be extremely aggressive and injury is always possible.

On another occasion Noon was with her sub-adult cubs in the grassy verges of Malik Talao. She had killed an enormous sambar stag and all morning each of her three sixteen-month-old cubs fed in turns. Noon carefully controlled the process to ensure there was peace between her cubs. From 7 a.m. to 11 a.m. I watched them feast when suddenly from the hills a volley of shrill sambar alarm calls rang out. Noon was alert. I drove off to investigate. A kilometre away Broken Tooth was pacing down the centre of the jeep track towards Malik Talao. I let him pass. He sniffed out a path that led him into the grass where Noon sat. I went back to Noon. She was frozen in a stalk position, completely alert with muscles rippling. Head slightly raised, she peered through the grass in the direction of what she knew now was an approaching tiger. The male cub had moved off. The two females sat a short distance away. Soon the grass rustled and Broken Tooth became visible as he approached Noon. In a flash Noon rose on her hind legs forcing the male to do the same and three bouts of a boxing match ensued amidst the most vicious coughing and growling. Both tigers ducked away from the punches. Neither was injured. Noon gave way, rolling on her back submissively. Peace descended as Broken Tooth approached the carcass to feed. After another half hour had passed the younger female cub couldn't stand it anymore. She slithered up to the carcass. At her approach Broken Tooth snarled, baring his fangs. Undeterred the young female nibbled on the edges of the carcass pushing herself in. That's how I left them at about 1 p.m. Sub-adult cubs are not tolerated near the carcass but when they are very young the father is much more tolerant.

As I have noted earlier, twenty months earlier Broken Tooth had mated with Noon but so had Genghis. We remain unsure to this day as to who fathered that first litter of Noon's. I had then watched Broken Tooth court Noon but missed the actual mating, which Fateh recorded. Fateh's diary reveals the magic of mating tigers.

For a week before their mating Broken Tooth and Noon were always together. It was like a courtship period and there was a constant sharing of kills, which Broken Tooth ate from first. At four o'clock one afternoon Fateh witnessed the tigers mating in the back pools of Rajbagh Lake. It was a stormy day and black clouds filled the sky. At 5 p.m. Noon emerged from the thicket and sat at the edge. Soon Broken Tooth appeared and sat a few metres away. Noon quickly got up and moved to the male, rubbing flanks and nuzzling him seductively before sitting down in front of him. Broken Tooth immediately rose and mounted her but a few seconds later she snarled up at him and threw him off. It was a spectacular scene as they were mating in the shade of a flame of the forest tree, its red flowers carpeting the ground. The tigers mated every ten to twelve minutes until the sun set. The remnants of a sambar carcass floated in the water and crocodiles sniffed the edges. Broken Tooth snarled at them but did not have the energy to pursue them. The carcass kept the mating tigers rooted to the edge of the water. In the distance a brown fishing owl took off. Two golden orioles fluttered across the sky, the bright yellow of their chest feathers providing relief against the dull forest green. It was nearly 6.30 p.m. when Fateh left. He had watched the tigers mate eight times in eighty-eight minutes. It was the first time he had seen mating tigers. Awed by the power and beauty of the scene he headed back as Broken Tooth snarled again at the crocodiles. For Fateh it remained one of the most important days of his life.

Young tigresses first come into oestrus between twenty-eight to thirty-six months. This is when conception can happen. Male tigers can father a litter from the age of forty to fifty months. A tigress who conceives may not come into oestrus again for eighteen to twenty-two months. If conception does not take place or if a litter is lost she will come into oestrus in one to three months. Tigers are induced ovulators—the female releases her egg only when mating has begun. The male tiger has a bone in the penis that stimulates the tigress, inducing ovulation. The penis has penile spines that induce this process and cause pain to the tigress who roars and tries to slap the male off her.

◆

The early 1990s were difficult times for Ranthambhore. Poaching scandals erupted and several tigers went missing, including Noon and Broken Tooth. There were widespread rumours about poaching, and by 1991, I was sure that the tigers in Ranthambhore were being poached. In 1992, a poacher was finally caught with a large tiger skin. I was shocked. I wondered how many tigers that I had watched and photographed had fallen prey to the poachers. Could Noon and Broken Tooth have been poached? We would never know. All we knew was that many familiar tigers were no longer to be seen. In a crisis situation governments tend to act without wisdom and sadly Jogi Mahal was closed down as a rest house as well as for visitors. The government felt that permitting people to stay there was a headache that they could not manage. Many of us launched a huge national and international campaign to put pressure on the government to take corrective action in Ranthambhore to save its tigers. Believing at the time that changes in government policy could provide the necessary relief, I joined my first federal government committee and over the next two decades served on more than 150 such committees. In 1992, I met the chief minister and senior government officials of Rajasthan and held extensive discussions. The first priority was to estimate the tiger numbers and finally in the summer of 1993 a comprehensive census of tigers was undertaken. My non-governmental organization, Ranthambhore Foundation, was invited to provide independent inputs as far as numbers were concerned. We created teams and worked the entire area of the park for ten days. I remember on one of these days I was tracking some tigers on foot at one corner of the park with the field director. It was extremely hot and the temperature must have been nearing 50 °C. Climbing up a hill I nearly collapsed and had to be rushed to the nearest forest post to be fed onions! I survived. From a combination of real-time sightings and pug marks we arrived at a figure of fifteen tigers. It was clear that a great tragedy had struck Ranthambhore. From a population of nearly forty-six tigers, the numbers had fallen to fifteen. The park management came up with a total of seventeen tigers. For the first time the assessments by both sides in the field were close. But there were obviously other forces at play in the state capital of Jaipur and the bosses there negated both counts on the pretext that it had rained and therefore both counts were in error as the tigers' pug marks had been wiped out. This kind of action is typical of our bureaucracy. Many committees were formed and much was promised but the recovery of tigers was a tortuous process.

Committees that were supposed to serve the tiger never really did and were full of hot air and endless chatter. Sadly I realized the futility of committees much later in my life and nearly twenty years after I first served on one. Committees neutralize the opposition and are used to do nothing but deflect criticism. In the 1990s I went to every location in India believing that I was contributing towards workable initiatives to save the tiger. I even created a huge network of non-governmental organizations and non-governmental individuals called Tiger Link in order to create collective strategy, but looking back I realize that I failed miserably and was fooled into overestimating my importance. Maybe some of my work helped keep a few of Ranthambhore's tigers alive, at least, I hope so.

We were lucky that one of 'our' tigers was still around the lakes. She was the original Machli, who was later called Lady of the Lakes. I profile her towards the end of this book. But this was a small mercy because overall the situation continued to be grim. My entire time was spent in campaigning in order to set this tiger paradise on the road to recovery. Sightings of tigers went down and it reminded me of the late 1970s when tigers were nocturnal. The park management was demoralized and the cattle graziers took advantage of this situation, filling the forest with grazing livestock.

Again I fought these negative developments and got several inspections done of the area by the federal government. I remember driving the director general of forests from New Delhi through the park one morning. He is the senior-most officer of the forest service; he was shocked to find graziers at every turn in the forest warming themselves around small fires and calling out to us as we drove by. Finding that I was not making much headway with the bureaucracy I decided to focus my work in the villages around the area and see if my NGO, the Ranthambhore Foundation, could make a difference.

Fortunately by now I had built a tiny house at the edge of the forest, which became my base of operations. At this time I noticed tigers leaving the forest and circling the edges of my property especially when the agricultural fields were lush and green. This gave the tigers good cover and they found deer and wild boar in the fields to prey on. The local farmers were happy because the tigers' presence kept their crops safe from intruding animals. This is when I saw a tiger confronting a wild boar, a tigress roaming around with four cubs and other tigers swinging by. I converted all my farmland into forest and luckily many of my neighbours did the same. This attracted tigers and still does. Two young orphaned tigresses spent several months in the area and even chewed my garden furniture one night. They were looking for goats and were soon relocated to Sariska Tiger Reserve.

The 1990s was the most troubled decade. Besides poaching, the illegal grazing inside the park reached incredible levels. This situation continued until 1996. Things began to get better after that. Much of the credit for the revival of Ranthambhore at this time goes to G. V. Reddy, who was appointed director of the park in the late 1990s. He was passionate, committed and led from the front and created the security so necessary for tigers at the end of the century. But the 1990s also saw some species vanish forever. The sarus cranes that used to frequent the edges of the lakes were gone. During this decade two wild dogs had arrived singly and even survived a few years but now they were gone. Ranthambhore was known to have packs of wild dogs fifty years ago but they soon declined as forest corridors between Rajasthan and Madhya Pradesh eroded. At the end of the century there were no viable corridors and for a wild dog to enter this area was near impossible. Another vital extinction that occurred was of white-backed vultures. They have gone forever and scavenging is left to a handful of other species of vultures such as the Egyptian and long-billed vultures. Big males like Broken Tooth had gone by the early 1990s and new males were difficult to observe, but in the late 1990s a young and enormous male was seen in the Semli Valley. He was so long and muscular that when I first saw him I exclaimed 'bamboo' in shock, so Fateh decided to call the tiger Bambooram. The name stuck and by the late 1990s Bambooram was world-famous. When President Bill Clinton came calling Bambooram was there to greet him. Fateh had retired by then but was still given the responsibility to work with G. V. Reddy to supervise President Clinton's visit. When the Clinton cavalcade was forced to stop because Bambooram was stretched across the road, few believed that the sighting was natural. The truth is that this tiger had killed a stray buffalo three days earlier. Fateh knew the tiger would eat for a couple of days and during President Clinton's visit, he was sure that Bambooram would be cooling off in the pools of water around Bakaula. Bambooram went one step further. As he blocked President Clinton's cavalcade and lazed in the middle of the road the president's security contingent became worried as the sun was setting. They had to push in close to the tiger to get him off the jeep track. The cavalcade then encountered a tigress who attacked and missed killing a sambar! The tigers of Ranthambhore knew how to put on a show for their very special visitors. When President Clinton left the park it was dusk. I had been invited to the helipad to meet him. He was overjoyed with his tiger encounters and we chatted for a few minutes about saving the tiger before he boarded his helicopter. If the 1980s belonged to Broken Tooth, the 1990s belonged to Bambooram.

◆

The turn of the century was a difficult period for wild tigers across India. Huge hauls of tiger and leopard skins were made in Ghaziabad near Delhi. The rampant poaching served to meet the demand for tiger parts in China. In 2000 I gave up my role of running the NGO I had founded. I had worked very hard with local people for twelve years to resolve conflict and create some harmony between park and people, but had struggled to find genuine support with different government departments to strengthen the interventions that had commenced. Our bureaucrats function like yo-yos. If good people get posted to a department or location—and this is rare—then everything goes well but then sudden transfers take place and mostly unconcerned people arrive who bring your work back to square one. There are no long-term partnerships created between those who govern and the non-governmental sector. As a result you never achieve anything and just as you feel you are succeeding someone new arrives on the scene and negates all the good work. With a heavy heart I moved away from the organization I founded. I focused again on the tigers that had inspired me like nothing else on earth.

I remember at this time going to Panna in Madhya Pradesh where my friend and colleague Dr Raghu S. Chundawat was working on a tiger research project. He was about to tranquillize and collar a big male tiger and I was a part of the process. This was among the first few tigers to be collared in India. I would realize later that collaring for the sake of collaring was to become a dangerous exercise. I will never forget that moment when we approached the tranquillized tiger whose half-open eyes watched us. When he was completely sedated, I was able to touch the animal I loved for the first time in my life. He was huge and as Raghu worked on collaring him I absorbed the incredible contours of the tiger. Huge paws, much bigger than one can imagine while following a tiger, a head that is enormous and glistening teeth that are frightening. I was mesmerized by the sheer power of the moment. I touched the animal on the head and flanks and silently bowed my head to what still is the greatest inspiration of my life.

LAXMI—AN EXCEPTIONAL MOTHER

BY 1986 RANTHAMBHORE WAS THROBBING WITH TIGER activity. Looking back this was one of my finest years with wild tigers. On one memorable occasion I saw sixteen different tigers in a day, including three different families, three resident male tigers and two tigresses. It was like living in a different era. I remember once finding three tigresses at each end of Rajbagh Lake. Fateh was delighted. He had dreamt of such a moment and this dream had come true. A large percentage of the world's tiger visuals and behaviourial records originated from Ranthambhore at this time.

Our greatest desire was to see a tigress with tiny cubs aged between one and four months. We wanted to observe the bonding between mother and cubs. We had seen Noon's cubs at five months but the earlier period was altogether invisible. Laxmi would grant us a peek into this stage of a tiger's life. In the early 1980s she had moved to a corner of her mother Padmini's range between Lakarda and Bakaula, encompassing the valley of Semli. Our sightings of her were infrequent and in the first part of the 1980s she was evasive and elusive. I believe this was her basic nature as she had grown up in an environment that was heavily disturbed by humans. In 1986 she was nearly ten years old.

Early one morning in March 1986 we were driving through the Semli Valley. Laxmi had already parted with her first litter of two and was very difficult to see. I could only get flashing glimpses of her while she crossed roads or moved from one patch of forest to another. That day, as I turned a bend in the road, there facing me at the edge of the track was Laxmi. She sat very still, looking at me. At first I did not see what was around her. Suddenly I realized that three tiny cubs were peeping around a bush. I froze. Soon she relaxed and all three cubs came out to cuddle her. She licked them vigorously. The cubs looked about two months old. It seemed that this was their first encounter with a jeep. As she licked her cubs I realized that another aspect of the tiger's secret life was unfolding before my very eyes. The cubs slowly found her teats and she lay back to suckle them. This was for me a first. Their tiny feet pushed away at her belly stimulating the flow of milk, as they suckled furiously. Then after ten minutes they jumped around her head and stalked a butterfly in the grass. One of them jumped on her back and another pulled at her tail while she licked the third cub. I watched this family drama for a half hour. Tears rolled down my cheeks as a tangle of emotions exploded within. I had seen all manner of tiger behaviour in the course of my life with wild tigers. I had seen the kills. I had seen how they ate. I had seen the aggression, the power and the fierceness. Here I was witnessing the tender care, the devotion and a mother's love. Gentle, cuddly and loving, the tigress soon rose and led her cubs away. For the next three months it was their remarkable family life that completely captivated me. Laxmi was very much like Padmini in her basic temperament. Calm and mature looking I seldom saw her ruffled. She had a lovely deep colour to her coat, and a swagger as she walked the paths and roads. She never feared the resident male or even transients. She commanded respect. Nothing she did was reckless or risky—and underneath it all was the fact that she was an amazingly devoted mother.

The next morning I found Laxmi sitting in a grass patch 10 to 15 metres from the jeep track. Her three cubs surrounded her. One nuzzled her face, another rested against her back, the third watched us curiously. Very tentatively one of the cubs moved a little towards us before rushing back to the security of its mother. Soon the cubs turned to each other and began leaping into the air and knocking into each other. After every bout they rushed to Laxmi who licked and cuddled them and soon decided to lie on her side and suckle them. All three soon found the right teat and began to feed. I watched this remarkable spectacle for more than fifteen minutes. I have never seen such a display of love and warmth, such evidence of the strong bonding between a tigress and her cubs.

Over the next few days we encountered Laxmi's family regularly in the valley of Semli and after each encounter were able to get closer and closer. Laxmi slowly got used to us. After that she was never bothered by our presence or our cameras clicking away. Slowly the cubs got bolder and one of them—who was the most confident—even approached within one metre of our jeep. We soon realized that there were two females and one male cub.

One afternoon I found Laxmi just after she had killed a chital stag. She dragged it quickly up the rise of a hill and into thicker forest. Of the cubs there was no sign. In about ten minutes she came out of the forest and walked 100 metres towards a network of ravines. I decided to follow, taking the jeep off-track and cross-country. Laxmi approached a bend in the ravine and called out 'Aaooo' several times. As she turned the bend I drove to the edge of the hill to look down. Below us was a gorge 30 metres long and 10 metres wide, surrounded on two sides by a cliff and rock overhang some 20 metres high. There were two caves in the cliff face and the three cubs came rushing out of one of them. Dense cover carpeted the floor of the gorge and a large pool of water reflected the light of the evening sun. It was a perfect hideout. Amidst a great deal of squeaking and squalling the cubs greeted their mother with much nuzzling and slowly followed her out of the ravine, meowing plaintively, as if they knew they were being led to a feast. On reaching a clearing Laxmi settled down to lick her cubs, showing once again the intimate bonds they shared. They then strode off towards where the carcass had been left. I followed through bush and rock until I could go no further. As I watched through a pair of binoculars, I noticed that Laxmi had opened the rump of the spotted deer and the cubs were greedily devouring whatever they could. It was clear that the cubs were used to meat even before the age of three months. It is this diet of milk and meat that makes them grow so quickly. Adult tigers prefer to eat from the choicest portion of the carcass, which is the rump, and then slowly move towards the neck. Cubs, in their greed, attack whichever portion they get to first. While they eat they snarl, hiss and try to growl. It is incredible the variety that exists in the language of the tiger.

For the next few weeks Fateh and I spent many days watching the cubs in this delightful hideout, observing and documenting facets of their lives and recording events that we had never seen before. It was April and the onset of summer. While waiting for Laxmi the cubs spent much of their time soaking in the water and fighting the heat. Cooling off in water is essential when summer temperatures cross 40 to 45 °C. Hair, coat or pelage—the magnificent striped patterns—not only provide perfect camouflage but keep the tiger warm and protect the skin. The stripes of tigers are used to distinguish one from the other. In fact the body stripes play a vital role in estimating the population of tigers and are an important part of the science of counting tigers accurately. Each body stripe of a tiger is like a fingerprint and different from the next. A comparison of the body stripes provides the numbers; today cameras are positioned on forest paths and roads to get accurate statistics.

Other aspects of the tiger's coat are also fascinating. For example, fur traps air which is a poor conductor of heat, thus insulating the tiger's body to keep it at a temperature of 36 °C. The longer the fur the better the insulation and tigers in Siberia have much longer hair on the back and stomach and tigers in warmer climes like India have hair that is nearly five times shorter. A tiger's outer fur is protective and the underfur is fluffy and a heat retainer. Tigers shed their hair from winter to summer so that they can bear the heat. As we have seen, in Ranthambhore, when the temperature crosses 38 °C, tigers must soak their bodies in water to cool down as often as possible. The cubs learn to do this as they grow. In the hot weather tigers use their tails like sprinklers. They sit in the water with tail immersed and frequently flick the tail to spray water on their back. It is a remarkable sight to see.

For Laxmi's young family a bit of playing, some climbing and exploring and a lot of sleeping was their daily routine. Laxmi's days were spent searching for prey. Choosing the right bush, she would appear to be asleep but at the slightest sound she would be alert and ready to pounce on an unsuspecting deer. Several times we watched her bring portions of her kill to the cubs to feed on. Whenever this happened the cubs would bound towards her in great excitement, each trying to be the first to reach the kill. The cubs were now becoming more adventurous, exploring the small ravine which was their den, nibbling at twigs and branches, chasing partridges and hares, chewing whatever came their way, prodding at stones and boulders, and investigating any small movement be it of birds or even lizards. New sounds like the sudden booming alarm call of the sambar, which had frightened them earlier, would now be accepted and they would raise their heads to sniff the air. The raucous barking of a troop of langurs would keep them alert and motionless and the shrill call of the stork-billed kingfisher would arouse their curiosity. A whole new world of sight and sound was unfolding and these young ones were learning to interpret it. The remnants of bones around their den would attract a stream of king vultures and crows and their movement was carefully watched by the cubs. The vultures never tried to land as the gorge was too narrow for them to feel safe. Crows were chased away. The occasional mongoose that slipped into the ravine would quickly retreat because the smell of tigers was everywhere.

We also noticed the regular presence of a big male within these ravines. Could it be the male that fathered the litter? Did the male play a role in bringing up the cubs? In a few weeks we had our most startling revelations. Up until then there were no records that we were aware of that showed the presence of the male tiger in the first days after the cubs were born. It is a time when the tigress chooses the thickest area in which to deliver her cubs. Giving birth is a long, difficult and arduous process as she can deliver up to seven cubs. Complete devotion of the tigress to her cubs in the first days ensures their safety, but seeing the father with the young cubs is a dream and I do not think that such a record exists of the first few weeks of life.

This was the same period of time during which Noon had her first litter and Nalghati her second. I was at times lucky enough to see all the families in one day and draw fascinating comparisons. But we still were not able to record the role of the father figure. For a long time it was presumed that male tigers were a threat to young cubs and frequently killed them. Most believed that there was no father figure in the tiger family. I assumed this to be true also. But an encounter in the valley of Bakaula changed all that.

◆

Bakaula was the coolest place in the park. Full of water and thick green jamun groves, it was a favourite resting place for tigers in the day and especially in the summer. This is where President Clinton saw two tigers on his visit to Ranthambhore. The scenery around here is quite spectacular. Cliffs rise up around the water and it is a great place to watch both Bonelli's eagles and stork-billed kingfishers. I would spend many hours in the summer exploring it and it was here that Fateh's son Goverdhan and his companions witnessed an amazing interaction between a tiger and a leopard. Looking for beehives in the trees they suddenly spotted a leopard atop the branches. She appeared bothered and restless and looking around they found a young sub-adult up another tree across the nullah. The cub appeared even more restless, moving up and down the branches and nervously looking down. The leopardess called to her cub several times. The green bushes hid the fact that there was a tiger sitting at the base of the tree that the leopard had climbed. The cub could not contain its fright and seemed to be sliding down the tree, urinating in absolute panic. Within seconds there was a huge growl and sounds of splashing water. A peacock cried out in alarm and took off. Then an ominous silence fell before they saw the tiger sprawled over the carcass of the young leopard. The leopardess looked on helplessly as the tiger started eating and cracking the bones. The leopardess watched from the safety of the tree as her cub was devoured. It was another unique encounter that Ranthambhore had provided.

In the 1980s I spent a lot of time in Bakaula. After the lakes it was one of my favourite spots. If the lakes were very open, Bakaula was thick and green and cool. In the summer it was like an air-conditioned room. This is a spectacular time in the forest as the flame of the forest blooms. The tree turns a startling red, the ground beneath the trees is littered with fallen flowers and entire stretches of Bakaula, Kachida and Anantpura turn crimson. It was here in this red and green mosaic of forest that another window in the family life of tigers opened for me.

It was 1 May 1986. At the edge of Semli, in the gorge of Bakaula, Fateh came across the Bakaula male and Laxmi. They were sitting on the vehicle track facing each other. On both sides of the track were thick groves of jamun, cool, lush and green. The temperature was nearing 45 °C. The area around was dotted with pools of water. Laxmi rose briefly and nuzzled the male and then a few metres away flopped on the edge of the track. A pair of Bonelli's eagles circled above a cliff where they nested. I heard the chatter of a stork-billed kingfisher. Suddenly this tranquil scene was disturbed by the sound of a rolling pebble. Both tigers were immediately alert. Laxmi moved cautiously towards the sound and the male had his head up. A sambar's alarm call echoed across the gorge. Laxmi had been spotted and a sambar walked away up an incline with its tail up. Laxmi was too far off to attack, but the sambar's path was closer to the Bakaula male. He was crouched, muscles rippling, as the sambar approached. She was not expecting a second tiger. In a flash, the male took off. Six bounds and he was on the sambar, forcing it down and quickly gripping its throat. From around the corner, a jeep full of chattering tourists approached the big male who was in the process of choking the sambar. Surprised, he took cover behind a bush. The sambar was not dead and twitched with small spasms. Laxmi, who was not shy of jeeps, quickly approached and provided the finishing touches and began the tedious process of dragging the 180-kilogram carcass to thicker cover. The male watched alertly as Laxmi reached a small clearing. The tiger moved towards her and Fateh watched a spectacular tug of war. The male had a grip on the rump and pulled at the hind leg, while Laxmi at the neck pulled in the other direction. The carcass was stretched between them, the tug of war interspersed with vicious, low-pitched growls and snarls. Then, suddenly, with a Herculean effort, Laxmi pulled the whole body and the male several metres. Pulling nearly 450 kilograms left her exhausted and she released her grip leaving the male to drag the sambar away. Laxmi strode off to Semli and the den where her cubs lay. She emitted a low rolling call and was answered by bird-like squeaks from her four-month-old cubs. After much licking and cuddling with endless squeaks, purrs and grunts, she led her cubs back and they must have known they were going to a feast as they circled her and jumped around her flanks. As they walked they clambered up branches of trees and romped around joyously. Laxmi was taking them to the male tiger. Clearly, this was not the first time they were going to share a kill with their father. They soon vanished into the bushes and this remarkable encounter was also responsible for dispelling the belief that male tigers killed their cubs, especially in the first months of their lives. Yet again, the tigers of Ranthambhore were rewriting the natural history of tigers. Laxmi had opened up a wealth of information on the early family life of tigers and some of our pictures were the first ever of both male and female with cubs. At the same time, as I have explained in the previous chapter, we had witnessed Nalghati, doing much the same with her cubs and the big resident male Broken Tooth, who besides Noon, had also mated with Nalghati. We now had seen and recorded evidence of the big male as father figure. What we saw in the 1980s took on a completely different dimension a few years ago as yet another chapter was added to the natural history of the tiger. A tigress had died, probably of natural causes, leaving behind two three-month-old female cubs. The park management decided to hand-feed them in the wild. While doing this they noticed that every few days a big male's pug marks would appear and for a day or so the cubs seemed to engage with him. The father figure kept an eye on these cubs until they were twenty-two months old, allowing them to share his food and walk with him while he patrolled. Big male tigers in the role of mother! When the two females were finally sent to Sariska because they were becoming a nuisance in the buffer area of the park, preying on livestock, the big male roared for most of the night trying to find them.

This event repeated itself when another tigress vanished leaving three little cubs behind. Here, the big male did much the same. Even after they were grown up, the three-year-old male cubs would band together and follow the father around. I believe extreme events or extenuating circumstances can result in new patterns of behaviour and this is what some of Ranthambhore's tigers revealed.

Depending on the circumstances, it is quite clear that tigers can band together to survive even if they are males. These are temporary coalitions. Usually the male tiger's territory encompasses the home ranges of several tigresses and while patrolling his terrain he is likely to encounter them and even spend time sharing kills and relaxing. He could also have fathered more than one litter in his range. It is only when a transient male enters that the tigress and her little cubs feel threatened. This or any other threat forces the tigress to change dens and sometimes this can happen when the cubs are tiny. It was many years later that I saw a tigress carrying her cubs and changing dens. Those jaws and canines can be most awesome when used to attack and most gentle when used to carry tiny cubs to safety.

◆

The jeep is like a mobile observation post in Ranthambhore. Tigers grow up with it around and seldom feel threatened by it. Man on foot triggers an immediate response from tigers and they will either flee or attack. When on the trail of tigers it is vital to make sure that jeeps are well serviced and fuelled. A lack of care can result in strange encounters as I learnt. While we watched Laxmi's family we were also monitoring Nalghati and her cubs. One of my most amazing encounters with Nalghati's cubs was when they were sixteen months old and waiting for their mother to return from the hunt. They were sprawled on rocks a few metres away from us. I spent an hour watching them. The male cub stood on a rock looking down at us. The cubs usually remain rooted to the spot in which they have been left by their mother and, if you are lucky, you can spend hours watching them. At dusk as I got ready to leave the jeep would not start. I could not believe it. I was with a couple of friends and we had two tigers peering down at us. After ten minutes of trying I realized that we had run out of petrol and turned to my friends and asked them to get ready to walk back. I remembered how Fateh had done it once and we decided we would sing loudly as we walked home. Luckily we were able to hail a passing jeep which gave us a lift back. When Fateh's driver went to the spot to bring the jeep back he found one of the cubs was in the back seat and jumped off when the rescue jeep was only feet away.

As Laxmi's cubs grew we had many encounters with them. We observed the different stages of family life, especially the dominance of the cubs over each other and the strict hierarchy each sibling observed in relation to the other. One of my final glimpses of this family was when they were sixteen months old. Late one afternoon we found all the siblings at the Semli waterhole. They seemed to be anxiously waiting for the arrival of their mother. It looked as if she had been away for most of the day. After an hour the dominant male cub suddenly became alert and in minutes Laxmi appeared from behind the bushes. In a flash the cubs—now nearly her size—rushed to cuddle and rub flanks and then started the most amazing purring I have ever heard. This was the big greeting after a long absence as the cubs and their mother bonded. The purring was louder than anything you could hear on Bose speakers. For me, it was a truly memorable day so far as tiger sounds were concerned. My senses were overwhelmed. I could not hear the driver speak that's how loud the purring was. After nearly twenty minutes, all four sat around the waterhole ready to start another night. At 6 p.m. a group of chital approached the waterhole to quench their thirst. The cubs froze in their positions and Laxmi was fully alert. The chital had not seen the tigers. Their tails were up but on suspicion only. They were desperate to get to the water to drink. One step at a time, they walked slowly towards the water in between Laxmi and her startled cubs. With her head down Laxmi seemed to glide like a snake for a few metres and then one of the deer spotted her and an alarm call resounded, sending all the deer into a panic. Each tiger exploded into action. In the chaos and confusion a fawn became separated from its mother and headed in Laxmi's direction. In one leap Laxmi pinioned the fawn between her paws and grabbed the back of the neck. The poor deer squeaked and died. A stork-billed kingfisher took off from his perch, his blue wings glinting in the fading light. Picking up the fawn Laxmi carried it a few metres away followed greedily by all her cubs. She then dropped the fawn to the ground and sprawled on top of it. The fawn was barely visible below her body as she snarled at her approaching cubs. The dominant male cub settled in front of her, snarling back. Another female cub also settled next to her sibling. Then both cubs started a moaning sound like a never-ending howl. I had never heard this sound before. They appeared to be begging, but Laxmi snarled viciously at them and lifted the tiny carcass a few metres further. Now all the cubs were moaning non-stop. This went on for several minutes until two of the cubs decided to leap at their mother and cannonball her off the carcass. She moved off and the male cub snatched away the fawn and in seconds was behind a bush devouring it. There is no sharing at this age and the rest watched for forty-five minutes as he ate. When he was done he abandoned the carcass and began to eat grass. Many tigers do this in an effort to help digestion or to bring up furballs. It is a form of self-medication. In some cases the eating of grass helps to rid the intestines of parasites and worms. Tigers have shortened guts and meat can be digested much more efficiently and then converted to protein. It was nearly dark when they all moved off down the road. I watched this wonderful sight for a while before heading home.

By now, I had witnessed the early stages of semi-independence and a remarkable evening of vocalizations. It had been the most productive day in terms of sound and bonding. Tigers are not very vocal as a rule. Their low, haunting roar that echoes far and wide means either that big males are sounding out their territories and signalling to each other or females are in oestrus attracting a male. When tigresses have young cubs, they tend to squeak to each other in order not to attract attention. It is a bird-like sound and sometimes difficult to assess as a tiger sound.

It is around the age of sixteen months that the first

detachment in the relationship between mother and cubs occurs. This is also the time when the cubs get their permanent teeth. The tigress forces the process ensuring that her cubs are well prepared for their solitary existence in the future. Laxmi's cubs had started becoming more aggressive with each other now. This was especially true of the two females. Laxmi's absences grew longer but she would still lead her cubs to the kill. It was while she was absent that the two females would become really aggressive, circling each other and then suddenly rearing up on their hind legs to box each other or hiss viciously. The smaller of the females would normally submit by rolling over on her back. The male cub was now spending much time with the smaller female. I knew instinctively that the larger female would be the first to leave. Even Laxmi was less tolerant of her larger female cub. The young tigers were beginning to assert their highly individualistic characteristics. The father, the big Bakaula male, continued to interact with the family but now the big male cub would keep his distance. My last sighting of all three cubs together was soon after they were eighteen months old. It was late one evening in June. I found all three cubs lazing around the Semli waterhole. Of Laxmi there was no sign. Suddenly a sambar hind appeared from the rear with two young ones. The three tigers crawled into different positions as if ready to attack and then charged the deer. Within seconds they were out of sight in thicker forest. I moved the jeep around and discovered the male cub choking one of the younger deer, who flicked its tail a few times and died. It was the first successful kill by the cubs that I had witnessed, with all three working as a team. This is the final lesson in independence and I knew the male would soon be on his way. The breakup of the family would start soon. The youngest female would be the last to go.

These were very special times. There was a great spirit of freedom in the park and tiger densities were the best ever. Even thirty years later I have never encountered the activity I experienced in the 1980s. There were very few tourists and, therefore, very few rules that governed human movement. You could see tigers everywhere. By 1987, Ranthambhore boasted fifty tigers. Laxmi and Nalghati had revealed the story of the big male and his role in the life of the family. Until then, and I am talking about the last 600 years, since paper records of natural history began to be maintained—resident males were seldom seen and tended to be evasive and invisible. This could be the reason why so little was known about their fatherly role. Mistakenly regarded as cub killers, male tigers were seldom associated with family life. But the observations we made in the 1980s changed that perception. Ranthambhore had yet again revealed something unknown about tigers for the world to see.

MACHLI—THE LAKE TIGRESS

THERE WAS AN ORIGINAL MACHLI, SO NAMED BY FATEH because of a fish-like mark on her cheek. She was the Lady of the Lakes and in the monsoon of 1997 had a litter. One of her female cubs inherited her name and, by the turn of the century, her territory. Females can slowly push their mothers out and the new Machli did just that. She was queen of the lakes and in 2000 she had her first litter—two male cubs and one female. I believe she mated with the huge male tiger Bambooram, the tiger President Clinton had seen on his visit to Ranthambhore in 2000. But after the monsoon of 2000 I never saw Bambooram again and he vanished just like Genghis. Did he get poached or poisoned? Nobody knows but he left Machli a litter of cubs to bring up.

The dominant male cub was a real character. Confident and curious he became a star. He was very recognizable as he had a twist in his tail and was soon known as Broken Tail. While he roamed the lakes with Machli he would chase a variety of birds including woolly-necked storks in the water and attempt countless charges on lurking crocodiles on the edges. His siblings had a tough time coping with his energy. He was too precocious and the first to leave the family unit in early 2002. Just before he and his brother left I witnessed them being suckled by their mother. It was an amazing sight to see two full-sized animals suckling at Machli's teats. It was probably a gesture of bonding rather than anything else but unique to see. In all my years of tiger watching I never saw this sight again. Cubs of this size rarely get suckled since there is no milk in the teats. It was like a farewell and in weeks the cubs moved away from the mother. Broken Tail survived for a year at the edges of Machli's territory but his brother vanished. One of my last sightings of Broken Tail was on the main road to the fort where he encountered a big male sloth bear and, without a second's hesitation, raced after it with such ferocity and anger that the bear fled. This was in the summer of 2003. But Broken Tail's dispersal from the family unit was not without its problems. In the monsoon that year (July 2003) he got pushed out by the bigger males in the area and took to the road.

Even without a resident male, Machli had managed to keep her male cubs safe. She probably did this through a combination of seduction and aggression with the males that she came into contact with. I remember the day when a wandering male tiger whom we called Nick sniffed her out. He circled her and made an effort to mate with her. Machli would have none of it and as he sniffed the air and curled up his lips she attacked him ferociously with tooth and claw. Even as ear-splitting roars split the air I noticed how both animals never sank their teeth into each other and were even careful with their claws as they rolled over in great ferocity. It was Nick who moved off first with a little bow to Machli. She had won the round. As he walked off he had a limp from a deep claw mark on the sole of a pad. This aggression kept Nick a little away from the cubs but two months later Machli was seductively arousing his interest as she glided past his body and submitted. This time they actually mated but just once before Machli moved off. This bout of mating had nothing to do with conception but it was Machli's way of keeping this transient male happy so he would not threaten her cubs. A couple of months later her cubs had left and she was ready for Nick who had become a regular presence in her area. The fact that tigresses could seduce male tigers to keep their cubs safe was a remarkable and hitherto unknown behavioural trait.

Broken Tail took the road to the Darra Sanctuary in Kota. This epic journey of more than 150 kilometres must have been traumatic, as he had to skirt both villages and people. The last tigers in Darra had been killed in the 1960s. When Broken Tail arrived at a patch of forest in Darra, not far from the city of Kota, he found himself near a railway track and was run over by a superfast train. I could not believe it. Maybe he thought the train would stop just like the jeeps would do in Ranthambhore. The tiger is extremely intelligent and rarely gets struck by cars, trucks or trains. Because of his broken tail, news of his death travelled fast when his battered body was recovered. This is what can happen to young tigers that disperse and are then forced to survive among humans and patches of wilderness. During his lifetime Broken Tail was one of Ranthambhore's most filmed tigers and, along with Machli, acquired worldwide fame. Eventually a film was made about his last journey from Ranthambhore to Kota.

All the lake tigresses—from Noon to Machli, the Lady of the Lakes—I had observed were extraordinary animals and gave me great insights into the lives of tigers in the wild. My encounters with Machli were as memorable as the others. On one occasion, when we started out at dawn, we literally bumped into four tigers—a mother with her three sub-adult cubs—the minute we entered the park. We were on the edge of Rajbagh and that morning the tigers were feasting on a spotted deer which they must have killed during the night. Machli was fast asleep on a high bank of grass. The cubs were grown-up enough to get restless and soon decided to stroll around the lake. One of the cubs started roaring. The sound was mesmeric. Slowly they walked towards Mori, occasionally roaring and snarling at crocodiles in the water. A pair of Brahminy ducks flew over them and they continued walking. Machli in the meantime had risen and slowly followed her brood towards Mori. Four tigers on the move is a gorgeous sight. They ambled across to a masjid, an old ruin on the first lake. A couple of peacocks cackled in alarm as the tigers made their way to Choti Chhatri where I was sure they would rest until the afternoon.

It was with great sadness that I learned of the death of Machli on 18 August 2016, just as I was finishing up with the proofs of this book. Machli—what a beauty of a tigress! Yes, she was the most beautiful of all the tigers I have seen and a star of the twenty-first century. Even towards the end, when she was nearly twenty years of age, and blind in one eye and toothless. She had lovely stripes around her cheek and body, and was a striking presence who brought great joy to those who observed her. I saw Machli for the last time in June 2016 at the edge of the park just after she had brought down a goat. I was amazed that she could still choke and cut through the flesh of small animals with just worn-out stubs of teeth. Calm and even-tempered, she reminded me much of Laxmi.

Lake tigresses are forever alert to sound. I remember watching Machli one day at Malik Talao where she appeared to be fast asleep in the shade of a tree. We waited patiently for something to happen. Suddenly Machli became alert as her ears picked up sounds that we could not hear. Minutes later, from 200 metres away, I heard the ear-splitting shriek of a sambar. Machli was up in a flash and racing towards the sound. We followed and around the corner we found a sub-adult sambar hind caught by a crocodile who was trying to pull his victim into the water. The sambar shrieked in agony. In a trice Machli charged in, forced the crocodile to let go and then quickly pounced on the severely injured sambar bringing it down. She then dragged it to a thick and inaccessible area to feed on. One predator's actions had resulted in another predator's feast.

The tiger's sense of hearing is truly astounding. On innumerable occasions, while watching a tiger, I have seen it becoming alert ten to fifteen minutes before I could detect the reason. It picks up the sounds of animals early enough to assess what its next move will be. The tiger's hearing is its most highly developed sense. With large external ear flaps rotating like radar dishes it can not only pick up the sound but also pinpoint it. The ear picks up the high-frequency sounds made by prey rustling in the undergrowth and also low-frequency contact calls, neither of which can be heard by humans. It appears that tigers can communicate by infrasound—a soundwave below the range of audible sound. Combined with its sight and sense of smell the tiger is rather like a mobile radar. I have observed many of Machli's cubs follow her exact path hours after she had passed just by sniffing the ground in her wake. The nose of a tiger is shorter than that of most dogs and they have fewer olfactory cells or smell-sensing cells than dogs but they are experts at picking up each other's scents.

A weak monsoon in 2002 resulted in a severe drought with most of the waters of the lake drying out by the summer of 2003. Large tracts of land in the lakebed were now full of both spotted deer and sambar that grazed on the green grass shoots. I don't know whether this triggered the poaching gangs, but from 2003-05 Ranthambhore suffered again at the hands of poachers. The tiger populations that had recovered from 1993 and reached about thirty-eight fell again. Luckily we had a chief minister who meant business and I was on an empowered committee that swung into action. Hundreds of home guards and armed police were positioned across Ranthambhore's forest. The tigers were saved in the nick of time. Despite these protective measures we lost at least fifteen to twenty tigers yet again. But corrective measures were brought in to quickly restore the park. It was not just Ranthambhore that suffered. Sariska and Panna lost all their tigers due to poaching. On my recommendation Prime Minister Manmohan Singh set up a tiger task force to which I was appointed. Sadly, three members of the task force were ignorant about tigers and were more focused on people-related issues. The chairperson also seemed to be unmindful of the real reasons for this task force and the needs of the tiger. I tried my best to fight for the tigers' rights, but the ultimate outcome of this task force was disappointing as it failed to take the needs of the tiger into consideration. I was forced to voice my dissent. It was a moment of time when we needed a major anti-poaching operation across India as well as many more well-protected tiger landscapes. Both vital issues were not addressed in the manner they deserved and we ended up losing a great many tigers. Indeed, 2005–08 were some of the worst years for wild tigers in India. However, Ranthambhore recovered gradually and its amazing tigers continued to contribute to the world's knowledge of wild tigers.

One such contribution was a first in the world of natural history and was recorded on film for the world to see. It was Machli's first litter. When these cubs were nearly ten months old a remarkable event took place near the shores of Padam Talao and close to Jogi Mahal. It was related to me by my nephew Jaisal Singh. Machli and her three cubs were feeding on the remnants of a sambar at the edge of the lake. It was a hot day and the carcass stank. The waters of the lake had receded because of a drought the previous year. As a hot breeze blew an enormous crocodile got wind of the carcass and left the safety of the water to start his slow walk towards the smell. My nephew was watching Machli from the forest. Jaisal was unaware of the crocodile's approach. Suddenly Machli became alert as the prehistoric reptile lumbered towards her. She watched intently and when it was about 25 feet from her she attacked it. The 12-foot crocodile was taken completely by surprise. He could not get back to the safety of the water and now had to confront a ferocious tigress out to defend her cubs and her kill. The crocodile put up a valiant struggle with flailing tail and snapping snout but it could not match the agility of the tigress. She was half his size but they battled for nearly an hour. Jaisal filmed the encounter from behind a bush. Machli grievously injured the crocodile. The next morning the tigers were gone and a chunk from the crocodile's flank had been eaten. This was the first ever encounter between a tiger and crocodile in the wild to have been recorded. Ranthambhore's tigers were once more rewriting the chronicles of natural history. That dry season Machli killed three more crocodiles. The shortage of water meant that crocodiles were moving from one pool to another more frequently and this made them much more vulnerable to the tigers' attack.

Machli was quite comfortable in the presence of jeeps. She slipped in and around them and used them for cover especially while ambushing deer. Visitors loved her, especially as she was seldom aggressive. Through the first decade of the twenty-first century she became Ranthambhore's star attraction and had a huge following. Her area of focus was the lakes. Visibility here was excellent and she performed at will for the hundreds who came to see her. One of her spectacular encounters, which was also photographed, was with a big male tiger on a day when he had killed a sambar. While he was away quenching his thirst Machli decided to sneak in and feed on the carcass. The big guy did not like this and when he returned he confronted Machli. They both rose ferociously on their hind legs snarling at each other but after a few minutes Machli gave in and submitted with a little bow of her head, falling to the ground just as humans have done with kings and people in positions of power over the centuries. Peace descended without injury to either. Her ability to resolve conflict was remarkable. I will go one stage further and infer that Machli had preferences for particular male tigers. She kept miles away from T24 when he entered her area but enjoyed greeting T25 and even T28. Tigers seem to assess their preferences for each other based on the very different characters that evolve in their society.

Towards the end of the decade I had my most wonderful

day with Machli and her fourth litter. She had delivered this litter of three female cubs in 2006 soon after her third litter had dispersed. By now she had lost three of her canines and hunting was not easy—tiger's canines are essential tools for survival. Somehow, Machli managed to keep hunting very successfully. In 2008, the cubs were grown and ready to disperse. I entered the park accompanied by my wife Sanjna and my son Hamir. We heard that tigers had been sighted in Gular Kui, the lower reaches of the fort. I spent some time debating whether to go there knowing fully well that much of the tourist traffic would be around the tiger. We did end up going only to find Machli and one of her cubs above a waterhole. They looked as if they had eaten; the remnants of their kill lay in the grass. There were too many vehicles around so we moved off, intending to return later. When we did we found fewer vehicles and both tigers in the water. The cub soon left the water but Machli remained for another twenty minutes, cooling off. The cub was now restless and Machli rose flicking the water off her body and both tigers started to walk towards Singh Dwar. We followed them, the first in a long convoy of vehicles. The cub clawed trees, marked the ground, scampered around and tried to play with her mother, but she did not respond. The cub had a full stomach and was totally relaxed. As they arrived at Singh Dwar they crossed a gate painted with tigers and peacocks in folk style. This was an important junction for tigers, much like a border between their territories, and I was sure Machli would turn up the hill towards Jogi Mahal. She did. They were now on the road to the park and had brought all traffic—including two stunned motorcycle riders—to a grinding halt. Now mother and cub slid past our jeep and the cub marked a milestone that said *Ranthambhore 1 kilometre*. As they crested the rise below the ramparts of the fort they paused and jumped over a small wall that took them to the edge of Jogi Mahal. It had been a delightful morning following these two for nearly 4 kilometres.

We were to have tea with the park director at Jogi Mahal and arrived in a state of excitement at having seen the two tigers. We chatted with the director and park ranger on Jogi Mahal's balcony. Sanjna and Hamir went off to laze on one of the lower branches of the tree. Peace descended amidst a few peacock alarm calls. A langur jumped from the roof of Jogi Mahal to the tree. Minutes later I heard the pattering of feet and saw a herd of spotted deer scampering through the banyan tree. At the same time I saw Sanjna racing to the steps of Jogi Mahal with Hamir in her arms. My heart skipped a beat. I moved a few steps forward and then saw one of the tigers—the cub—bouncing into the tree near where Sanjna and Hamir were. Sanjna had moved instinctively, sensing the deer's panic even though no alarm call had been sounded. She had created the space for the tiger to walk in. As my camera clicked the first pictures ever of a tiger walking through the hanging roots of this ancient banyan tree I thought to myself, with great delight, that one of my long-held dreams, to see a tiger against the backdrop of the great banyan tree, had finally become a reality. Adrenalin flowed as the cub crossed the tree and went to the far side before vanishing. Now a cacophony of langur alarm calls filled the air as we began talking excitedly about this amazing event only to be interrupted by a chital call which punctured our conversation—we watched with bated breath as a tiger raced in pursuit of a chital. I managed to click two photographs. It was glorious.

I had a vision sometime in the 1980s of waking up in the middle of the night and looking towards the banyan tree from my room window and seeing a tiger slip by. To this day I do not know whether it actually happened or whether it was a dream. Right now I was beside myself with delight. Suddenly one of the jeep drivers said, 'Tiger coming back.' I rushed forward on foot to the corner of the tree even though the director tried to stop me. I knew that there would be a fleeting opportunity to take an unforgettable photograph. I clicked just as the young tigress retraced her steps, calmly and slowly walking past the hanging branches and roots of what has to be one of the finest banyan trees in India. I continued to click while walking a few paces with her, my heart pounding. For me this was it. The magical forests of Ranthambhore had produced their finest vision.

◆

It was on that same trip that we were able to observe the conflict that starts within a family when the cubs reach a certain age. One day, we found Machli and her cubs in Kawaldar, a gorge that leads into the Nalghati Valley. Machli and one of her cubs were resting in the shade of a tree growling ferociously at each other. They seemed to have had a spat. We moved on a little ahead as I suspected that the tigers would start to move. A few minutes later the forest trembled with the ear-splitting roars of tigers. They sounded really furious. Such aggression is rarely seen. Ten minutes later both tigers walked along the road towards us but an angry mother suddenly turned on her daughter and they rose on their hind legs to box each other with their paws. I had witnessed such a boxing match just once before when a female tigress tried to stop a male tiger from usurping her kill. It looked as if the moment of separation was around the corner. For Machli the cubs had grown too big and were a real nuisance in terms of demanding food especially as they were now capable of killing smaller animals. As they walked down the Nalghati Valley a few metres apart they passed a roadside labour camp. Pots, pans and road materials lay on the side of the road and the cub sniffed all of it before moving on. Behind us the sound of another jeep revealed the presence of another cub walking behind the first two. One hundred yards separated the tigers as they walked past us. Machli branched off towards the forest and suddenly the second cub raced at full speed towards the first one. The forest was split open by one of the most ferocious confrontations I have ever seen. The two female cubs were snarling, hissing and growling and with such intensity that it completely overwhelmed the senses. For nearly five minutes they reared on their hind legs and boxed each other. Machli watched the confrontation quietly. The two females were asserting themselves against each other and I was sure that in a few weeks they would be ready to leave Machli and fight for territories in their mother's range.

The next day we were informed that Machli and her cubs were around the Rajbagh Lake. We could not find them but I discovered the Lakarda tigress lying by the edge of the lake. A descendent of Padmini's, this tigress had moved 5 kilometres to the areas of the lake from the hills of Lakarda. She was small in size, very confident and eager to explore the lakes even though she was entering Machli's realm. It was clear that the two adult females and three sub-adult females were circling each other amidst lots of aggression. The young and fit Lakarda tigress was asserting herself in this territory. She soon rose and roared loudly making sure that she was heard by all the other tigers around the lakes. Maybe all this ferocious roaring was an effort to dislodge the reigning empress of the area, Machli. But this would not happen without a fight. Even the sub-adult cubs would play their role as it would be in their interest to take over their mother's territory. While this was going on, the big Lakarda male was engaging with all these females some of whom would become his future harem. This huge tiger patrolled an area of at least 50 square kilometres across the Semli Valley and Bakaula and the hills of Berda. Little did I know then that the state government would pluck the Lakarda tigress out of Ranthambhore and airlift her to Sariska Tiger Reserve where poachers had killed all the tigers. This single act would seriously disrupt the lives of the Ranthambhore tigers.

By now the Rajbagh Palace had been completely taken over by tigers. Its cool underground rooms and shade attracted tigers in the summer. It was also a great vantage point from where to plan attacks. I started to call it Machli's palace. Indeed, many locals believed that Machli was the reincarnation of a past queen. After all in the good old days the palace had been a pleasure garden where fountains played and the royal retinue relaxed. Today, no one has the courage to enter. The rooms inside the palace were full of bones and though I spent much time there in the 1970s watching birds, I would hesitate to enter it now. Today, the wilderness has encompassed it making it a true tigers' den.

Tigers slid in and out of it daily. Out of the four chhatris on each corner, two had been brought down by the weight of trees and branches. The front entrance of the palace touched the water and Machli would often wade to it snarling at the crocodiles. The cubs would play in the pavilions and chhatris and climb the overhanging branches as they flexed their limbs. I have even seen the resident male enter to spend time there with the family. Once, in 2009, Machli's sub-adult cub was lazing around in one of the chhatris. In their never-ending quest for succulent plants, sambar grazed in the shallow water on the edge. One of the sambar began approaching the corner where the tiger rested, unaware of the predator's presence 16 feet above. The splashing alerted the tiger. It crouched, and as the sambar came into range, the tiger leapt from the chhatri bringing the deer down and into the water. After a brief struggle, the sambar succumbed. The sub-adult dragged it out to feed. It was truly a palace kill and something I have never seen again.

◆

For me such encounters are the stuff that dreams are made of. Sunset on the lake. Tigers jumping out of palaces to kill deer. If Jogi Mahal was not a day shelter, with a chowkidar guarding it, the same scenes would be happening there. I know that the staff there have watched Machli and her cubs explore the terrace and balcony of the structure and mark the edges with their scent as if they owned it. Another favourite spot for these tigers was an ancient gate close to Jogi Mahal which had a room towards the top. Machli would enter this room and peer out. A board nearby said, 'Protected Monument, Archaeological Survey.' If only they could see how effectively their monuments were being used and protected! Choti Chhatri and Badi Chhatri were great vantage points and nearly every ruin was used by the lake tigers. The old masjids were sometimes used as day shelters and this connection between the memories of man and the tiger was more than magical to observe. These ruins framed the tigers who sat in them just as they must have humans centuries ago.

Machli enjoyed taking her cubs down the main road below the ramparts of the fort. One afternoon in 2008, while we were driving to the main entrance, one of her cubs was strolling on the road. Of Machli there was no sign. She was probably a few hundred metres ahead. The cub was very confident and carefully sniffed and marked the 1 kilometre milestone. As she moved away a motorcycle carrying two adults and four children approached from the other side. Six people on one motorbike! For a moment the tigress, the motorbike passengers and all of us in the jeep were frozen in shock. What on earth would happen next? Then, realizing their predicament, the man leapt off his bike and started running backwards with his family. Worried about abandoning his bike he called out to us to bring him the keys. The tigress watched. Little children running on the road ahead some 50 feet away from her did not affect the tigress's cool demeanour. She continued walking, pushing all oncoming traffic into reverse, creating complete confusion. She then left the road and we saw the man rushing back to retrieve his bike and move towards the fort to pick up his family. The tigress returned to the main road a few minutes later and walked on. At the same time the man with the motorcycle was returning with his family believing that the coast was clear. Seeing his error he rapidly retraced his steps. I noticed that the seat cover of his motorbike had a fake tiger-stripe design. By this time we were in splits of laughter in the jeep. Where on earth could you witness a scene like this? Only the tigers of Ranthambhore could be as gentle as they were with such human activity.

The years from 2007-10 were difficult times for Machli. Many tigers were being picked up from Ranthambhore and taken to Sariska Tiger Reserve and this was having a negative impact on Ranthambhore's tiger population. The big male of Ranthambhore was lifted out and younger males competed for the lakes. During this upheaval pretend mating may have helped Machli to keep her cubs safe. When a tiger tried to get aggressive she would retaliate with such ferocity that the male normally left the arena limping. Machli also disliked sloth bears but they were too large for her to bring down. My only recollection of an encounter between her and a bear was when she fled from a charging bear up in the hills of Kukraj. Bears are formidable opponents and can stand their ground even when confronted by a pair of tigers.

Leopards who lived near the fort bore the brunt of Machli's anger. Once I saw her poised under a tree with a leopard cowering above. She kept him there for an hour before ambling away. Leopards generally fear tigers and often get killed by them. Machli's daughter T19 not only killed a leopard but carried it in her mouth to her cubs and then allowed them to sniff at it without letting them eat it. Usually leopards are not devoured. A chunk or two is plucked out and then the carcass is abandoned. Similar behaviour has been recorded when tigers kill hyenas. Machli was also a great hunter in the waters of the lake. As we have seen, she had no fear of the crocodiles and had killed a few of the big ones.

When nearly ten tigers were relocated to Sariska the dynamics of the tiger territories in Ranthambhore changed completely. I am not clear on how exactly it affected Machli, except it was around this time (2010) that she was pushed out of much of her old territory by her daughter T17. She lived on the edges of Malik Talao and Lakarda. By 2012 she had no canines but still managed to chase and kill her prey. She did this by choking her prey; she would keep her grip on them for up to twenty minutes as her canines could not do the job. This is when pressure was applied on the park authorities by those who wanted this star tigress to be immortal. Soon Machli's diet was supplemented by live buffalo baits. Slowly this queen of the lakes got relegated to a small ravine in Lakarda. There was a lack of grace and elegance to the process. One of Ranthambhore's finest was being kept alive for the world to see but in completely unnatural circumstances. Should this be done? It is becoming a fashion across the world. Scarface, a large male lion in the Masai Mara in Kenya, nearly lost his eye in a fight with another lion. A skilled eye surgeon was found to operate on his eye and save it. But I am against such interventions.

Sometime in early 2015 Machli moved to the ridges very close to my home and that is where she spent her time eating live baits and walking past my home every week. She would also take shelter in three or four resort hotels in the area where vegetation was thick. One of my last encounters with Machli was in October 2015. I heard from the forest guards entrusted to monitor her that she was in a patch of grass a few hundred metres from where I live. We walked towards her in high grass. I could see no sign of her and believed she would slip further away. And then with a roar and an angry look towards us Machli leapt up, turned and trotted off to a nearby hill, jumping easily over an 8-foot-high wall. I was truly impressed. Here was a nineteen-year-old tigress who was still amazingly agile and aggressive to human intruders on foot. Later that evening I watched her walk across the hills amidst booming sambar alarm calls. Soon she started roaring and the hills echoed with her calls. There was a half-moon up in the sky and I wished her luck on her next journey. Less than a year later she was gone, but she will live on in the hearts of her legions of fans.

Twenty years is a long time to share with a tiger and many of us will miss her sorely. She had an aura that enveloped the beholder. What can we all learn from her life? Work with a unity of purpose, protect precious tiger turf across the country, intensify rigorous field science, create innovative public-private partnerships that keep our wilderness safe, outsource areas for management and partner with local communities to minimize damage. Can we do it? Yes, but only if there is a mindset change in both bureaucrats and politicians. The time for shuffling files is over. Machli's passing is the end of an era and a new generation of tigers is waiting for a new and dynamic policy that will keep them safe.

T24 OR USTAD—THE UNPREDICTABLE ONE

T24, OR USTAD AS WE CALLED HIM, WAS BORN IN 2006 to a tigress then called T22. Most believe he was part of a litter of three with one male and one female sibling. I twice had a glimpse of the mother and both times I saw only one cub. The area that T22 and her cub roamed in was Lahpur and Guda. This huge range, which encompassed the edge of Sawai Madhopur town and Ranthambhore right up to the fort, had probably the highest tiger density in the region. During the period that the cub was growing up the forest administration was busy shifting tigers to Sariska. As I have said earlier, I believe the tigers in this area suffered serious trauma as a result of losing nearly ten tigers to Sariska. This upset the natural balance and forced new interactions. T24 was a victim of this trauma. He was the toughest and most aggressive tiger that I have ever known. He always put me on my guard whenever he looked at me. His very nature was domineering and I think most other tigers preferred to stay out of his way.

The first time I encountered him was in March 2009 as he confidently walked along the road in Zone 7 on the edge of the park. I must have followed him for 2 kilometres that day as he spray-marked trees and bushes and raked his claws on the bark. At a young age he was asserting his territoriality and, unlike other tigers, would look you straight in the eye. I knew then that I would have to watch this tiger carefully. What I did not know then was that he would become the most dangerous tiger Ranthambhore had ever known. At this point in time he was nearly three. In April 2009 he was found limping and the local forest department tried to treat him by first tranquillizing him and then applying ice packs to the injury. In the process they held him captive for more than forty-eight hours. They got a veterinarian who normally dealt with cows and buffalo to give him antibiotics for the small wound in his forepaw. This is now a common practice across India. The forest authorities also got the field scientist to radio collar him. One can only imagine the trauma T24 went through. I was told later that even while he was tranquillized and being treated, he suddenly sprang up and ran off into the bushes. It has become the fashion nowadays to tranquillize and treat ailing tigers, but it was highly unusual in those days. The collaring process takes no more than thirty minutes and the animal is immediately released. In T24's case, the treatment took two days. All in all it was a most clumsy operation. It is no wonder that T24 was traumatized by the experience.

I saw T24 once more after the monsoon of 2009 in the area in which he had been radio collared. He looked as big and strong as ever but this time a collar hung unattractively around his neck. The Wildlife Institute of India was trying to obtain information on young male tigers and how they disperse. I have never come across this information. If it exists it has probably been filed in some dusty drawer. This young male made forays into the area around Sawai Madhopur town and was seen a few times even close to Fateh's farm. On 3 July 2010 Fateh called to tell me that a young male tiger had killed a man near his home. The tiger had a collar. I was stunned. Even when the locals shouted at the tiger to frighten it away, so they could retrieve the body of the man, the tiger refused to budge. It took a lot of effort to move him. There were very few cases of tigers killing humans in Ranthambhore. I asked Fateh if the tiger had begun eating the man and was told that he had. I told Fateh that this tiger needed to be relocated to a captive enclosure in a zoological park but Fateh and the local forest officers wanted to give T24 another chance. I was not convinced and voiced my protest. T24's victim was Ghamandi Mali, who was cutting wood on the edges of the forest.

A week later the big resident male of the area was airlifted to Sariska and the vacant range was quickly filled by T24. Man was interfering with the entire balance of tigers. A young, aggressive, man-eating male tiger had the run of an area full of human beings as well as the entire Ranthambhore road that pilgrims use to visit the Ganesh temple and the fort. In the monsoon of the same year T24's radio collar, which was probably of poor quality, stopped functioning and in November he was tranquillized once again to remove it. He was forced to undergo the trauma of, quite literally, being manhandled, once again. I could well understand his growing distaste for humankind.

T24's home range varied between 30 to 50 square kilometres. In Ranthambhore the range of the male can be as small as 5 square kilometres or as big as 150 square kilometres. It seems to depend on the density of prey. Males prefer areas that have more females and since females prefer areas that have greater food the males manage to get both! In Siberia, where prey concentrations are low, males can have extraordinarily large territories of 800 to 1,200 square kilometres. In Ranthambhore young male tigers from the age of twenty to fifty months remain in transition and are like drifters looking for a different bed each night.

Sometimes they have been known to walk 30 kilometres in a night and can range over 200 square kilometres. In comparison, young females either settle into their mother's range or push their mother out.

In the winter of 2010, and throughout that season, I would encounter T24 each time I was in Ranthambhore. I often came across him on the main road to the fort and once even on the road that links the town of Sawai Madhopur to the park as he sniffed around some of the resorts in an effort to prey on livestock. Many of my encounters were in the Nalghati Valley and in the pools of water that lie at the edge. Here there are crevices that he used to cool off in. He would also rest in the shade of trees and bushes just below Phuta Khot, which is known as Ranthambhore's mini Colorado with its towering cliffs that reach for the sky. On other occasions he would be found walking on the Sultanpur track. He was very comfortable with jeeps and I never experienced either an attack or a mock charge. However, I always warned my family that this was a dangerous and unpredictable tiger and we needed to be totally alert in his presence. I will never forget T24's eyes, which literally drilled a hole in you. My favourite track on which to follow him was behind the fort on the Khemsa Kund road. This was a narrow track that ran alongside a gorge with the awe-inspiring ramparts of the fort on one side and thick dense forest on the other. Banyan trees dotted the area. When T24 walked here he stuck to the road. Being off the tourist track there were no other jeeps; this was also one of his favourite day shelters.

In the forty or fifty times that I encountered T24 he would be marking trees, or scrape-marking the ground in order to leave his signal in the area. He was one of the most prolific markers that I have come across. Tigers of both sexes turn their hindquarters towards any elevated spot such as a tree, bush, patch of grass or rock overhang and with tail raised vertically shoot out a pungent spray of fluid hitting the target at an upward angle. The fluid is a mixture of urine and a secretion from the anal glands and is very musky and has a strong odour. In some cases, especially where it has not rained, the smell can last up to forty days and is an excellent indication of whether an area is occupied or how recently a tiger has passed. This may encourage or discourage tigers and repel or attract conflict. After ejecting this spray tigers will often sniff it and then hang their tongue out with nose wrinkled. As I have noted earlier, this behavioural response, known as flehmen, occurs when tigers sniff another tiger's scent. The smell conveys a wealth of information for tigers, such as the age and sex of the owner, and whether or not a female is in oestrus. Cubs can follow their mother via the scent, and the scent of a tigress in oestrus will pinpoint her position for a dominant male. Areas are also scraped and secretions from a gland between the toes enable the cubs to follow their mother's footsteps. There are scent glands in the tail, around the anus and in the cheeks and chin. T24 did much rubbing of his cheeks on barks of trees and frequently rolled in patches of grass to leave his scent behind. I have watched a tigress sniffing the scent of another tiger and quickly retracing her steps. Territoriality is an integral part of the tiger's life.

T24 also provided remarkable encounters with the natural world of Ranthambhore. One of these unique events was recorded by the local expert and naturalist Aditya

'Dicky' Singh when he found T24 courting a female at the far corner of his range. It was 9 April 2011. A mother sloth bear with two little cubs on her back wandered by the pair of tigers. The tigers went alert; the bear did not realize her predicament. Suddenly, she saw the tigers and froze. The cubs slipped into their mother's fur. First, the tigress moved rapidly forward to confront the bear, who rose aggressively on her hind legs, her lethal claws a warning. The tiny bear cubs were now invisible in their mother's fur. The atmosphere erupted in the most blood-curdling coughs and snarls as tiger and bear faced each other but the bear did not give way. She was protecting her cubs and her aggression was so vicious that the tigress was forced to retreat. Now it was T24's turn to charge and he did so with a roar but the bear snarled back, ready to attack with her paws. T24 could not match the bear's ferocity and was forced to retreat. The bear never flinched and slowly walked away. The tigers watched. Sometimes tigers do kill bears but by and large they prefer not to engage. On this occasion the tigers may have been too preoccupied with their courtship to attack successfully or the bear was too aggressive for them to take a risk. Whichever way you look at it, it was yet another remarkable event in the natural history annals of Ranthambhore.

Fateh also witnessed a few encounters between tigers and bears. On one occasion a sloth bear was feeding on the fruit of a tendu tree. A tigress stalked towards the tree but the bear saw her and came rushing down and charged her. They both played hide-and-seek for a while until the bear departed. On another occasion a bear was shaking the branches of a ber tree to dislodge the fruit. As he fed from the forest floor a tiger crept up and both tiger and bear reared up on their hind feet to slap each other. They did this thrice until the tiger got fed up. Both soon went off in different directions. But Fateh's best encounter was when two tigers were feeding on a sambar kill and a bear passed by. The tigers charged but the bear stood its ground and started approaching the kill forcing both tigers to retreat. One of the tigers charged, roaring loudly, but the bear retaliated by rising on its hind legs. The tiger moved back and the bear annexed the carcass. The second tiger made no attempt to go for the bear.

In Ranthambhore there are very few fatal interactions between bear and tiger. The only one I know of was caught on a camera trap—in this encounter, a big male on the edges of the park killed a bear cub and walked off with it dangling from its mouth.

◆

In October 2011, when I arrived in the forest, I realized that there had been an exceptional monsoon. I had never seen Ranthambhore so lush, wet and sparkling. Water flowed from every corner and I soon discovered that it had rained more than 1,200 millimetres—nearly double the normal amount. The dry burnt forest had turned an astonishing lush green and all the dry streambeds were gurgling with water. It was unbelievably beautiful. It was in this emerald forest that I had a memorable encounter with T24. I received a message on the wireless that T24 had turned off on the Khemsa Kund track in the non-tourist zone. The forest glinted in the rays of the early morning sun. The road became a shaded path as the branches of the trees on either side of the forest closed overhead. The steep walls of the fort loomed on our left and an even higher cliff towered on our right. We were rooted in history. It was from this cliff that Akbar, the Mughal emperor, had attacked the fort of Ranthambhore and laid siege to it for more than a year.

As we wound our way upward we saw T24 strolling down the road nonchalantly. We followed him for nearly a kilometre, watching him mark trees and bushes and rearing on his hind legs to rake the bark of a tree. As I have mentioned before, these territorial signals are important after the monsoon as the rains have wiped out the scent of tigers. Those who have retained their territories are busy re-marking them. T24 suddenly swerved off the road and as we inched forward we realized that he had decided to stop. He watched us with his cold stare. He was near a pool of water and a tiny waterfall trickled down behind him. The emerald forest did not just frame him but embraced him from each side. He was a flash of orange in a tangle of green. After an hour we left him to rest and headed home. Sadly, this tiger was slowly pushing Machli to the edges. I believe she did not like him and preferred to keep out of his way. As we have seen, she ended up being pushed close to my home.

Big males like T24 do not necessarily have a long reproductive life. A male tiger may be capable of mating and fathering cubs even before he reaches the age of four or five, but he seldom gets the chance to do so. By that age he is in his prime, strong enough to take over territory and protect the females that go with it. Yet his active reproductive life will last only a few years before he is ousted by a younger male. The reign of a male tiger in Chitwan, Nepal, lasted only four years but he had seven females in his territory and succeeded in siring twenty-seven cubs in that time. A female in the wild does well to breed and survive until the age of fourteen or fifteen. Machli survived longer as she was given food to eat. Most male tigers fare rather worse, dying at the age of ten or even younger because of the frequent territorial struggles they must endure.

◆

On 9 March 2012, T24 killed again. Ashfaq Ahmed was collecting ficus leaves for his livestock about a kilometre from the spot where T24 had killed his first human victim. T24 devoured most of this latest kill. Sadly, Fateh had passed away by then and I tried my best to convince the authorities to pluck this tiger out of Ranthambhore either alive or dead. I knew that T24 would become a huge problem if action was not taken. But the chief wildlife warden decided against it. It was a flawed and regrettable decision. Even the National Tiger Conservation Authority (NTCA) remained non-committal on this issue. The ignorance of our decision-makers is truly abysmal. I warned one and all that T24 could attack again. And he did so on 25 October 2012. This time his victim was an assistant forester inspecting road repair work after the monsoon in an area where jeeps ply regularly. His name was Ghisu Singh and I had met him several times. He was pounced on while walking on the road and dragged to a bush. Even though the road workers raised an alarm by shouting, T24 did not move an inch. Even after most of the forest department arrived he continued to retain his position near the body. In the end three jeeps with racing engines had to move him off and retrieve the body. T24 snarled but when more than twenty people retaliated with noise he finally moved off. It was quite clear that T24 would have eaten Ghisu's remains had he not been kept at bay. He was already a confirmed man-eater and this was my worst nightmare coming true. Still the chief wildlife warden took no action and the NTCA wrote a letter stating that the tiger needed monitoring but stopped short of saying he should be removed. I tried again to convince the authorities that this tiger had to go. It had tasted blood. Again my pleas fell on deaf ears. T24 was getting famous and the bureaucracy seemed to get a vicarious pleasure in letting him remain on the loose. Shouldn't the bureaucracy have been held responsible for the death of three humans? And for perpetuating the reign of this man-eating tiger? These were important questions that needed to be asked, enquired into and answered. But nothing happened, the matter was soon forgotten and life in Ranthambhore went on as usual. I was certain there would be another attack. In the meantime, T24 was observed by numerous tourists and became a star. He rarely charged jeeps and the hundreds who were ignorant of tiger behaviour were happy to believe that he was a tiger who intended malice to no one.

I knew by the end of 2014, from my old group of forest guards, that they were wary to walk in his area. One of the forest guards had even been stalked by T24 but when the guards accompanying him made a noise and banged their sticks, the tiger moved off. The forest guards were uneasy. Few wanted to patrol or walk in the area. I had never encountered anything like this. In my early years I would happily walk all around the park tracking tigers. There were few places that I had not seen on foot and we never had a worry about being charged or attacked. There were no tigers like T24 around. I remember tracking tigers in the most inaccessible gorges at the height of the summer without any concern of being attacked. The only thing that attacked you was the heat! If tigers like T24 had existed no one would have gone out tracking and forest patrols and the other staff would have been demoralized.

In the middle of January 2015, people noticed that T24 was looking unwell; between drivers and guides they created enough pressure to once again force the forest department to interfere. The officials decided that T24 was constipated and needed an enema! So, once again without thinking, they tranquillized him and proceeded to stuff him with medicine and antibiotics and injected soapy water up his rectum. I could not believe it and again insisted that this must stop. This tiger was being traumatized repeatedly by his so-called well-wishers. His problems continued and when I saw him in February he was thin and listless. In the tigers' kingdom it is the survival of the fittest. Some make it, others do not. It is not man's job to enhance their lives by medical treatment. Tiger reserves are not zoos. But it has become difficult to explain such logic to people. By March T24 somehow recovered, was no longer constipated and started following his normal routine.

On 8 May 2015, while I was in Jaipur for a meeting of the State Board for Wildlife chaired by the chief minister of Rajasthan, we heard the horrendous news of T24 attacking a forest guard I knew well, Ram Pal Saini, who manned the entry point to the park and monitored the traffic that went to the fort. That evening the horror story unfolded. About 200 metres from the main gate, Ram Pal's wife had spotted a tiger near the water. She was collecting grass in an area in the buffer zone and tigers seldom sheltered there because of the proximity to the outside villages and the ticket gate for tourists. She informed her husband about the tiger and three forest personnel, including a forester, walked down the tarred road to investigate. It was 5.35 p.m. Ram Pal was on the path behind the other two men. T24 was hiding in a bush and as Ram Pal came within striking distance he pounced and killed him instantaneously by tearing apart his neck. As T24 stood over the body a car drove by. This was the main tarred road to the fort used by one and all. The car's occupants noticed the tiger standing over a body and used their horn to force the tiger away. Within minutes the other two guards had called for help and both forest jeeps and Aditya Singh and Dharmendra Khandal, a wildlife scientist, arrived. The body was brought out by using several jeeps to keep the hidden tiger at bay. Ram Pal Saini was rushed to hospital but was declared dead on arrival.

At the spot where he had made his kill T24 suddenly came out of the bush. Watched by many people, he spent several minutes searching for the body and sniffing at the blood. His actions were caught on film. He then calmly walked back into the forest through Mishadara gate. One of the jeeps following him had to brake suddenly, causing one of the passengers to fall out. When T24 heard the noise he rushed towards the jeep. Luckily the person was able to jump back in. As night fell the tiger turned into Sultanpur and continued his leisurely stroll. This time there was a general consensus that the tiger had to go and this united stand was supported by the chief minister of Rajasthan.

Within a few days, in a highly efficient operation,

conducted as temperatures soared to 40 °C, T24 was sent to the Udaipur Biological Park and is housed there today in an enclosure. Instead of people supporting the departure of T24, and condoling with the families of the dead, all hell broke loose on social media. The gist of the protest was that an innocent tiger had been sent away and this was the doing of hoteliers and others. I have never seen such abuse showered on people like Aditya, Dharmendra and even myself. Overnight a movement sprang up to bring T24 back. The local villagers and forest guards were having none of this and wrote letters saying that if this tiger was returned they would stop work or go on dharna. Most of the media supported the return of the man-eater. Much misinformation was spread. A group of T24 supporters went back and forth from high court to Supreme Court, but finally the high court ruled that the decision to send the tiger to captivity was the right one; the Supreme Court upheld the decision.

Protestors on social media insisted that all T24's cubs would be killed by the new male who would take over. No one mentioned the fact that there were only two male cubs that might have been fathered by T24 and they were already sixteen months old, making the possibility of the cubs suffering a tragic fate unlikely. In the end nothing happened and in fact a new male was observed in October 2015 sitting with both the mother and the now fully-grown cubs—three males and a female, all together.

The uproar over T24 pointed to the general ignorance in society at large, as well as the media, about tigers and their ways. Campaigners protested on the streets of our cities and ran poster campaigns and billboards supporting the return of T24. Candlelight marches were held. I watched aghast. I wondered what had happened to these protestors on social media when numerous tigers were taken to Sariska. Did they open their mouths about the impact of that move on cubs or breeding? Where were they during the deepest of crises in Ranthambhore's history? I wish we had the same energy to fight poachers and poor governance. Yes, it was possible that the foolhardy actions of the forest department and others had traumatized a tiger and created a man-eater and corrective action was necessary to prevent unintelligent interference in the life of wild tigers in the future. But to perpetuate the myth that T24 was innocent was ludicrous to say the least. By October 2015 this tamasha was over. The protests fizzled out when those protesting saw pictures of T24's victims.

◆

The period from 2007-15 was a difficult one for the tigers of Ranthambhore and a strange moment in the park's history. I know for sure that there was much more conflict between man and tiger during these years. T24's lifespan coincided with the relocation of tigers to Sariska. How did one affect the other? It is difficult to say for sure but I believe that it might have had something to do with T24 turning rogue and killing four people. At least six other people were mauled in the park by other tigers during this time. Even Machli, without any teeth, attacked a goatherd who tried to save his goat from certain death. In October 2015, a young tiger attacked a man near Ranthambhore road.

As I've said earlier in the book, in my opinion, the relocation of the Lakarda tigress followed by many others not only upset the balance and reduced reproductivity but also made tigers angry. The forest departments had a great lesson to learn from these unfortunate events. I hope that one day they will learn to take informed decisions instead of treating tigers like cattle. All of us—and this includes my conservationist colleagues who first get emotional and then irrational—need to introspect about T24 and learn from that experience.

I stated the facts for the media: this tiger was a man-eater. He had to go. I had never been so viciously vilified on social media ever before. Without his departure no forest guard was prepared to patrol the park on foot. This could only have encouraged poachers to move in. The local villagers threatened to burn down the park if T24 was not removed. Near anarchy would have resulted. It was a time I lost touch with both friends and conservationists. I believed that those who were trusted colleagues needed to accept my view—after all I had observed Ranthambhore's tigers for forty years. When it comes to man-eaters it is important that the view of local experts, specialists and the forest officers are taken into account, especially if they are all in agreement. This is not a debatable issue. It is about human life. A stalking tiger interested in human flesh is like a monster in a forest and has to go. The job at hand is not to save individual tigers or artificially keep alive the star tigers of a forest. Our job is to keep the breeding habitat of tigers safe and ensure that there is sufficient prey for them. If that is done, tigresses will produce litters, and hopefully wild tigers will thrive.

I have touched upon the fact that there are important lessons to be learnt from T24's saga. Wildlife institutes in India and elsewhere need to refine their methods of collaring and uncollaring animals in order to avoid traumas induced by humans for tigers. Human interference in the tiger's life—be it by treating injuries, illnesses or constipation—should be prevented as much as possible. The silent expert members on different bodies and committees need to speak up on the issue of relocating normal tigers. More than 20 per cent of Ranthambhore's tigers were shifted to Sariska and no one protested even though none of these were strays as Ranthambhore has never had strays. It is almost like an island that tigers exit from only for short periods of time. In the forty-year history that I know of, two tigers went to Kuno in Madhya Pradesh, two went to Kota and Bundi, one got run over by a train, one went to Bharatpur, one to Datia and a few more into the ravines around the Chambal. In the period when Sariska was being repopulated no one bothered about the tigers that were outside the park. They were too difficult to find and dart so they chose the easy way of capturing them from deep inside, causing havoc in the tiger's realm.

◆

One of the most fascinating observations of T24's life was his very individualistic behaviour. His brother T25 was totally different. Calm and gentle he never showed aggression. The only time he exploded with anger was when he encountered T24. Then they fought viciously but, by and large, T25 preferred to keep out of T24's way. T25 was a remarkable character. He lost one of his tigresses when she was tranquillized and treated with antibiotics for a small wound that had become infested with maggots. It was yet another foolish decision. The tigress died a few days later leaving behind two female cubs aged four months. The forest department immediately moved in to feed the motherless cubs little realizing that T25 had become both mother and father for them. T25 would walk them in his range, share food with them and visit them once or twice every week to ensure their safety. This went on until they turned into adults. The two cubs, known as B1 and B2, were frequently given goats to eat while they were growing up and ended up at the edges of villages around the park waiting to attack more. They even managed to chew the garden furniture at my home and were finally plucked out and taken to Sariska.

T24 would never ever have the grace of T25 and a lot of that can be put down to the experiences he suffered at the hands of man. The nature of tigers is shaped by their traumas. T24 suffered from being captured and collared. He lives today in an enclosure in Udaipur. He is nearly ten and will pass away in the not too distant future. No other tiger anywhere should be subjected to the traumas he went through. Even in his captive state at Udaipur he has had serious intestinal problems and faced a major surgery to relieve his pain. No effort is being spared to keep this animal alive. I do not have a problem with that, but hope very much that we all learn from this experience and ensure minimal interference in the lives of wild tigers. T24 was tranquillized four or five times by the park management and associated scientists. In the process he was not just traumatized but became unpredictable and aggressive. It is vital that we do not make the tranquillizing of tigers into a fashion. These days at the smallest sign of injury tigers are tranquillized and stuffed with antibiotics. This is ridiculous and must stop. If there is anything that we need to learn from T24's story it is to interfere only when absolutely necessary into the natural life cycle of tigers. In Ranthambhore we need more behavioural observation without invasive techniques. After all most tigers in Ranthambhore allow you to watch and follow them.

Fateh always said—let them be free—some will live long others will not—that is nature and it is not man's job to play God to them. Let our wilderness be really wild and not manipulated by man.

T17, T19, OTHER TIGERS AND THE FUTURE

MACHLI'S BIGGEST CONTRIBUTION TO RANTHAMBHORE was in 2006 when she produced a litter of three female cubs. Female cubs are vital and assist in the health of the population of tigers as they regenerate. At the time when the cubs were getting ready to leave their mother in 2008, Ranthambhore was sending its tigers to Sariska. To adjust to this man-made interferences, as we have seen, both male and female tigers had to do much adapting and moving around. I have said this before, and will say so again—this, in my opinion, affected the breeding of Ranthambhore's tigers. As a result, the sex ratio got skewed resulting in more male tigers than females. So Machli's cubs in 2008 were really precious and valuable. Machli's three cubs were given many names but were generally known as T17, T18 and T19. Machli at this point was referred to as T16. T17 was the most dominant of all her siblings and exceedingly confident around jeeps. She knew how to use the jeep as cover and one of the best experiences of this comes from Aditya Singh who described T17's encounter with a jeep. 'To our surprise she then started stalking directly towards our vehicle. She was moving very slowly to avoid being detected. When she almost reached the vehicle she lifted her head to check the deer who were unaware of her presence. In fact the deer were moving in closer to the vehicle and T17 went flat on the ground right behind the rear wheel of the vehicle and stayed there for what seemed like ages. She then crept into a shallow ditch at the edge of the road. I would never have thought that a fully-grown tiger could squeeze into it and be concealed.

She crawled in slow motion to the other end of the ditch and within 25 metres of the deer. Realizing she had to now attack she charged out of her hiding place and hit a female spotted deer on her hind legs. The deer flipped into the air but the tigress' speed had taken her too far. She overshot and as the deer regained its footing it fled. The tigress looked away in annoyance.' From the heyday of Noon, tigers have used jeeps as cover to get close to their prey. Cubs learn this art of stalking around vehicles to perfection. T17 was excellent at it.

From 2008 onwards T17 slowly pushed her mother Machli away to Lakarda. Soon after, in 2009, her sister T18 was taken to Sariska. T19 remained at the edges of the lake but by 2010 she was walking into the Lahpur Valley and keeping away from her sister. T17 had by now taken over as the lake tigress. The following year was a difficult time for me. Fateh, my best buddy and tiger guru, was diagnosed with cancer and died on 1 March 2011. An era had ended and the man who had for forty years sacrificed his heart and soul for wild tigers was gone. Somehow the tigers knew it and while Fateh's body lay in the house at the edge of the forest a tiger roared incessantly at 4 a.m. as if in mourning.

◆

In late October 2011 when the forest was a lush green, I watched a dainty and delicate chinkara pick its way up the hill near Rajbagh. My reverie was rudely interrupted by the crackling of a wireless set. T17 had been sighted on the main road to the fort. The traffic had jammed and I decided to go to Jogi Mahal knowing that she would jump in from behind the banyan tree. The lake was filled to the brim, the peace extraordinary as a crocodile glided through the water. Two bronze-winged jacanas were at the edge of the lake. The scene was disrupted by the barking alarm calls of the langur. T17 was on her way. I jumped into the jeep and found T17 crossing near the gate onto Butterfly Lane at the edge of the fort. We saw her framed by the ancient gate. The sunlight made patterns on her coat and then she vanished into the thick monsoon vegetation. The langurs were calling further away and we drove on. Butterflies and grasshoppers flitted around and little migratory birds of prey, kestrels and falcons, zipped around in the lush green canopy. Every crevice was filled with water.

T17 had a penchant not only for Jogi Mahal but also the fort. In all these years I had only on one occasion seen a tiger on the fort. As I have mentioned, tigers avoided the fort because they were disturbed by the endless stream of pilgrims going up and down. Leopards would slip in and out and even walk on the fort walls but tigers were rarely seen. T17 changed all that. It was the fourth day of the new moon when thousands of pilgrims circled the fort hoping that Lord Ganesh would grant them their wishes with the support and blessings of all the other gods. As the pilgrims wound their way up to the fort they found T17 sleeping on the path. She did not budge for hours. The traffic of pilgrims on foot had to be stopped.

This was a time when I was in mourning for Fateh, lost in my thoughts and memories of the big-hearted tiger man who was my closest friend in the world. Some of us had scattered his ashes across the forest, which was his last wish. But even as I mourned him, it seemed only natural to be following T17 around. I was sure Fateh was watching from somewhere with a smile on his face.

T17's cubs—two males and one female—were born in the early summer of 2012 and she spent the first months with them around the lakes. Her sister T19 had a litter before her in 2011, probably fathered by T28, and raised her cubs in the hills of Kukraj, adjacent to the lake, and the valley of Lahpur. She was a clever and elusive female, very different in temperament to T17. Both sisters, T17 and T19, kept to their home ranges, seldom overlapping even though these areas were adjacent to each other.

Then, one day in early 2013, something very strange happened. T17 and her cubs left for Kachida and the edges of the park near Badlav, some 10 kilometres away. I could not believe it—T17 left the best area of prey density in the park for a dangerous place, on the edge of the forest, where the locals were unfriendly and prey minimal. And she did this at a critical point in the cubs' upbringing. I had never witnessed anything like this before. Most believed that the males T25 and T28 had overlapping territories and T17 took to T25's area as he had fathered her litter. But since she had mated with both I felt it would have been impossible for her to conclude with any certainty who the father was. It didn't seem a theory with any merit. Did her sister T19 push her out? The park was in a mess because of the Sariska transfers. In any event T17 did not last long. She vanished. Most believe she was poisoned by villagers on the edges of the park near Badlav. Her orphaned cubs were ten months old and had to be fed and then helped along, as we have seen, by T25. They survived. T25 seemed to be a remarkable male tiger. For the second time he engaged in the cubs' upbringing and this time even tolerated the two male cubs ensuring they reached sub-adulthood. These cubs are still together roaming the forests of Kachida and Bakaula. The female cub is seen sometimes in Kachida and Badlav.

Once T19's cubs dispersed, T19 seemed to be taking over the area around the lakes. Her presence after the monsoon of 2013 was becoming more and more regular around the lakes and Jogi Mahal. One day, in early 2014, T19 appeared with four cubs near the gate just beyond Jogi Mahal. I had seen at least eight litters of cubs born in this dense patch. Machli was born here and had her cubs here, and now both T17 and T19 had used this as a first den. A new queen was back ruling the place she was born in. When the cubs were two months old, in the summer of 2014, T19 walked all of them to Machli's palace. She had to clutch them in her jaws one by one as she waded through the water. The crocodiles watched. Another saga was about to start in the life of Ranthambhore's tigers. Ten days later, when T19 exited from the palace she had only three cubs with her. The crocodiles' revenge maybe?

T19 became the resident of the lake and 2014–15 was some of the richest tiger time I have ever seen on the lakes. The best of it was seven days from the end of May and to the beginning of June. Unlike T17, T19 had two female cubs and one male cub. It was strange how the sex ratio became skewed following the relocation of tigers to Sariska. Sometimes there were so many males in an area that they would chase single females around. Ranthambhore suffered for seven years and it was only in 2013 that some normalcy was restored as the tigers readjusted their territories and filled vacant ones. The presence of T19 and her cubs was the best thing that happened in the area around the lakes in 2014. The cubs grew under the tutelage of their mother and were typical lake tigers. My long encounters with them started in early 2015 when they were big enough to be a nuisance and swept across from one lake to the other. They would range from Malik Talao to Padam Talao trying to attack everything in their way from sambar to chital and even a sounder of wild boar. One day, in the panic created by their lake walk, T19 managed to kill a chital fawn which was snatched away by the male cub who then feasted in solitary splendour. Then all four disappeared into the palace for a siesta, emerging at 4 p.m. The water in the lake was still high and they swam across, snarling at the lurking crocodiles. For me it was a delight. In all those decades I had never seen four tigers swimming across the lake.

The cubs were learning to deal with the huge reptilian predators that infested the lakes. Snarling and trying to charge crocodiles on the edge of the lake were all a part of their training. Like their ancestors they would turn into expert crocodile killers in the future. The foregoing took place in early March. By the time I returned at the end of May the cubs were just over fifteen months old. They seemed much more independent than I would have imagined. The male and one of the females would stick together. They had created a coalition. And one female would either be alone or with the mother. Sometimes around the lakes a distance of half a kilometre would separate the cubs. They would all be drawn together in the presence of the mother.

One morning while they strode across Malik Talao I watched the two female cubs in a vicious engagement. One went for the other rising up on her hind legs, amidst ear-splitting growls. T19, who was sitting 50 feet away, raced in to separate the cubs and prevent injury. Using her paws she mock-slapped both, pushing them away. It reminded me of a parent separating two squabbling children or a teacher doing the same in school. A few hours later in Rajbagh much the same happened and T19 once again leapt in to separate her daughters. It would be tough going and I knew one of the female cubs would soon disperse.

On three occasions during this trip I witnessed the fresh presence of a leopard near Jogi Mahal and each time because of T19 or her cubs it was treed. On one occasion T19 found a spotted deer killed by a leopard that she scavenged with her cubs. The leopard watched the proceedings from the treetop. Leopard-tiger interactions are rare and a treat to watch. I find the intense dislike that tigers have for leopards astonishing. Tigers will go out of their way to tree leopards and then sit below the tree for hours hoping the nervous leopard will clamber or fall down. I knew of a case where a big male tiger treed a leopard and was so angry that he clambered up the tree in pursuit. Luckily the leopard remained on the top and on a branch the tiger could not get to. The tiger descended, annoyed and angry, and circled the area for hours before leaving. One day T19 was seen carrying the carcass of a young leopard in her mouth and dropping it for her cubs to sniff at and investigate. She did not allow them to eat it.

Tigers usually do not eat leopards. On another occasion the Bakaula tigress, a large shy animal that frequented the area of Bagda-Bakhola and Semli and slipped in and out of this lush green habitat, sniffed out a spotted deer kill in the heart of Bakaula. It was where a leopardess was tending to her three-month-old cubs in a depression in the cliff face. As the tigress started climbing towards the spot the leopardess managed to extract one cub in her mouth and rapidly move off. The tigress arrived, caught the second cub by the scruff of his neck, shook him and killed him. She then proceeded to carry him in her jaws and vanish into the thick jamun bushes of Bakaula. I have known of ten leopards that have been killed by tigers and innumerable examples of tigers chasing them to tree them. Leopards in Ranthambhore keep far away from the tiger.

◆

On several occasions T19's family strolled around Jogi Mahal. One morning, at about 9 a.m., the female cub was moving around a lot and finally took the path to Jogi Mahal. We followed. Over the years the great banyan tree that loomed over the area changed shape with two big branches collapsing. Usually tigers circle this tree from its rear rather than walk under it. That is exactly what this cub did. We watched her circling the back of the tree and then pulled our chairs to relax under the shade of the tree. The forest was silent for a few minutes as paradise flycatchers flitted in and out of the branches. A pair of golden orioles flew across when suddenly we heard a shout, 'Tiger coming.' A second cub had turned towards Jogi Mahal. As Sanjna and Hamir got into the jeep I remained seated on a chair under the tree with my camera. I was alone. The second female cub came padding along. I watched as she paused at the tree debating whether to go behind it or through the tangle of its branches. She looked at me and started walking towards me and the tree. She came strolling to within 15 feet of me as I stood up clicking away. She watched me and marked the edges of the tree. I thought for a moment she would climb the branches. But no such luck. Peacocks called and watched her from the branches. She glided around the enormous roots and slowly vanished to the other side. That banyan tree of Jogi Mahal is a part of my soul. When tigers walk under it, it is an intensely spiritual moment for me.

In October of the same year I got a message that the same sub-adult tiger was walking on the fort road just like her mother T19 used to do. I rushed to Jogi Mahal to await her arrival. Within minutes she came striding past the tree. It was the third time in my life that I had seen tigers walking through the hanging roots of the tree. The next day, T19 was leading her cubs into Jhalra. All four tigers were walking below the ramparts of the fort when the male cub flushed a hare. As the hare took flight he chased it across a wide area for just under a minute. What a sight! Shades of the cheetah.

◆

Fortunately, the richness of Ranthambhore's tiger experiences gradually erased the bitterness that had enveloped the tiger world over T24. It was certainly true in my case. I saw nine different tigers on my trip to the park in 2015. My field diary of 4 June reveals the magic of our encounters. 'At 5 p.m. at the edge of Rajbagh watching T19 and her two cubs. They all look hungry waiting for a sambar kill that could satiate their appetites. The setting sun glances off Machli's palace. The female cub strolls towards her mother who snarls and then slaps her away. She flops to the ground. A crocodile glides away at the edge of the water and the cub snarls at it viciously. The sun sets and I know that in the monsoon, less than a month away, this family will disperse.'

Another generation of tigers was getting ready to find their new homes and lives in the enchanting forests of Ranthambhore. When I arrived there after the monsoon, T19 was still around and frequently followed by her male and smaller female cubs. The larger female kept to herself. She was very aggressive both with mother and sibling. I followed her for a while one afternoon as she lazed around Choti Chhatri. She watched a group of chital pass her. A woolly-necked stork was feeding at the edge of the water. I must have seen this scene a hundred times but the excitement remained at the same pitch every time. The chital moved closer. The tigress froze. She slowly stalked forward on her belly—gliding like a snake. Her tail flicked up and down. The chital quenched their thirst and started to leave the water's edge. One of the fawns veered away and was now 10 feet closer to the tigress. As the fawn stepped closer the tigress flew off the ground and in a blur of motion brought the fawn down. The chital herd shrieked in panic. The mother of the fawn tried to get closer, calling out in panic, and desolate at losing her baby. It was one of the female cub's first kills and would give her great confidence in the life that awaited her. She decided to carry the spotted deer to some thick bushes where she fed for an hour.

All the lake families—from Nick Ear and Noon to Machli—always made the palace on the edge of the lake the focus of their lake activities. They would enter the palace by wading through stretches of water. During the day the young cubs would laze in the chhatris or in the arches that looked out over the lake. Sometimes they would cool off in the abandoned lower rooms. They would exit from a gate that faced the back of Rajbagh, walk to the tall grass and slowly to Malik Talao. For forty years I have watched them all use much the same paths and tracks.

◆

In my lifetime I must have seen nearly 250 different tigers all over India. At least 125 of these were in Ranthambhore and many of them were observed over long periods of time. I made a detailed study of at least seven to eight tigresses with four cubs, twelve tigresses with three cubs, ten tigresses with two cubs and only once a tigress with a single cub. Such were the reproductive successes of Ranthambhore that most of these cubs survived to the age of two—it was only after that that many vanished, either because they were unable to find new areas within the forest and were therefore forced to go to human-dominated areas where they were poisoned or poached or because they were killed by other tigers who would not tolerate them. I believe that the sub-adults who vanished were mostly poached by man.

In these forty years of tiger watching there were some observations and inferences that I made. I have shared many of these in the pages of this book, and in my other books, and as we come to the end of my narrative I'd like to share just a couple more. One of these concerns the ability of tigresses to avoid mating with their sons and the ability of brothers not to mate with their sisters. Looking at the records of the last thirty years I do not know of even a single case where a tigress mated with her son. It is only while putting this book together that I realized that this could be one way in which incest is prevented and genetics strengthened. Male cubs move far away from their mother's range whereas female cubs push their mother outwards and take over her range or adjacent areas. Even though the lake area in Ranthambhore is one of the best for prey density there is not one case of a male tiger asserting his presence if his mother or sister was resident. These males grow up in these areas and yet leave them irrespective of the quality of the area. Dr Raghu S. Chundawat, who studied tigers in Panna, had similar observations on this issue. Based on my observations I believe males move out from their mother's range and keep out of her area in her lifetime. As they reach sexual maturity they attempt to take over new areas but not in their mother's or sisters' range. This prevents direct incest. Many male tigers leave the home range of their mother around the age of three and never come back. In fact, I do not know of any instance of a male cub in adulthood returning to his mother's area. Look at the case of Sultan or T72, son of a tigress called T39, and believed to have been fathered by T24. Sultan was a massive male, more than three years old and tolerated by both his father and mother. In fact, T39 had a new set of male cubs and permitted Sultan to spend time with them. Two weeks before T24 was picked out of Ranthambhore, Sultan moved into Kela Devi Sanctuary 25 kilometres away. He was not pushed out by anyone. He just left. He is still there. The area has little prey, much human disturbance and he lives on livestock kills. In 2015 he had been there for seven months and would soon become sexually mature but far away from his original birthplace and mother's area. There is only one case in Ranthambhore of a brother and sister trying to mate without any conception resulting. It is clear that there is a natural process that occurs where direct incest is avoided as far as possible between male and female cubs.

Females mate with the resident male but if they can they slip away to find adjacent male tigers to also mate with. Sometimes when they are forced to confront transient males they seduce them and mate with them but no conception results. This process resolves conflict and could play a role in enabling the tigress to protect her cubs from these male tigers in the future. Male tigers do not harm their cubs if they think they have fathered them and females can therefore create much confusion among males on this issue. As I have said earlier, when T24 was plucked out of Ranthambhore many believed that what were considered to be his sub-adult cubs (both males) would be attacked by the male that replaced him. But in October 2015 the cubs were seen happily sitting with the new male who had taken over from the adjacent area. Had T39, the mother, also seduced this male at some point? This area of inference is fascinating. All the six orphaned cubs that were hand-reared and fed and survived until adulthood were tolerated by both resident males and females. Are some tigers more territorial than others? Is being territorial an individual characteristic? Are some tigers more tolerant than others? In Ranthambhore tigers do much overlapping into each other's areas. The ranges they use shift and change, expand and contract. This change also occurs in drought and other seasonal factors.

The issue of fathers mating with daughters is a much greyer area as resident males can be fooled into believing that they have fathered the litter when actually they have not. Again, from my experience, fathers keep away from their daughters and successful reproductive mating is rare.

This is a fascinating area for any young scientist to work on and reach inferences. As far as the territory of male tigers is concerned, I have found great overlaps with adjacent males creeping in to mate with females or to hunt, especially when a resident male is in another corner of his range. How well defined, then, is the range of a male or are there several other males that transgress but live in an orderly way based on dominance? Submission at the right moment of time can resolve conflict and this may be the case especially for small isolated areas like Ranthambhore.

Conflict over these last decades has been at its highest levels between adult females and sub-adult sisters as they fight to retain either parts of their mother's range or adjacent areas. These conflicts can be vicious and can cause injuries. Compared to conflict between males or even between male and female siblings or adult males and females, conflict among females as against males is at the ratio of fifty to one. Males move away as sub-adults and fight much less even within a litter. The big males resolve conflict easily as less dominant animals submit. It is the females that clash often. I have seen many more rows between females and much greater injury inflicted by them on each other. T19's two female cubs were vicious with each other and were not just scolded by the mother but also separated frequently by her. Still, she could not prevent these sub-adult females from gashing each other regularly. The aggressive attitude of the female is not lost on the big males that walk Ranthambhore. They are very wary of the resident tigresses and I personally witnessed a big male walking away limping from a fight with Machli. Tigresses are probably even better hunters than tigers as they have to hunt much more while raising their cubs. Their predatory abilities are unquestionable and the big males are mindful of this.

I am often asked what qualities make for a good tiger mother. As far as I am concerned, it is her devotion to her cubs until they leave. I remember watching T19 in 2015 as she walked past Malik Talao causing much panic among the sambar and chital deer. She walked behind a slope and when she reappeared on the other side she had a sambar fawn gripped in her mouth. She must have surprised it. Her cubs were now nearly eighteen months old and could have made such kills on their own. But T19 walked to the edge of a gorge where she left her victim behind a bush without eating even a morsel. She then walked down the gorge to Lakarda, about a kilometre away, calling loudly. She was calling her cubs in to feed on this tiny animal. It is this attitude that makes for a successful mother. She found her cubs after much roaring. Her male cub took his time to follow her back to the kill. But each time he deviated to either watch or stalk other animals she would patiently sit and wait until he came back, both calling to each other incessantly. In the end it would only be the male who would snatch this fawn away and devour it but they would all wait and watch him feasting. T19 did this repeatedly with her kills, ensuring food for her cubs as long as they remained with her. When the issue of supplying food is the prime focus, a tigress will ensure the survival of the litter. Just like humans there are warm and affectionate mothers, and cold and detached mothers. The same is true of tigers. This probably also holds good for the male tiger that fathers the litter. The Bakaula male and Broken Tooth were tolerant and patient fathers but I would not say the same of Genghis or T24.

Another inference over my forty years with tigers concerns the ability of tigers to recognize specific human beings that they encounter. In the 1980s, both Fateh and I spent long periods of time watching tigers like Noon and Laxmi. Fateh would at times sing and talk to them. I always held that they had an affinity to him with his distinctive build, Stetson and guttural voice. I know that tigers recognize their own kind and, therefore, the possibility of tigers recognizing specific individuals seems very plausible. The memory of this remarkable animal has been completely underestimated. Their short-term memory is said to be thirty times better than that of humans and they do not forget easily. After all, tigers do have one of the largest brains amongst carnivorous animals, second only to the polar bear. In the 1980s, after watching Noon nearly every day for twenty days, I sometimes felt that she was able to recognize and assess the jeep and its human occupants who watched her.

I am not a scientist and can only speculate on some extraordinary events and behaviour that I have seen. Another inference that I have drawn based on my observations is that the behaviour of tigers is highly individualistic. I have seen more than a hundred tigers in Ranthambhore's forests and each one developed its own character. Genghis and Broken Tooth were complete opposites as were Laxmi and Noon. Different techniques of hunting, tolerance and raising families were clearly evident as each tiger slowly developed characteristics depending on its experiences of growing up. One of my abiding discontents has to do with the attitude of the forest staff in Ranthambhore to findings of people like myself, who after many decades of observations in the field come up with insights that deserve proper scientific investigation. Rigorous field observations can shed light on hitherto unknown aspects of the tiger's life. Such studies need to be encouraged.The tendency of forest administrations is to discourage field research of any kind. They discourage so-called outsiders—that is anyone who is not forest staff to do any kind of work within the forest; non-governmental people who have the freedom to work inside are also not wanted. It is felt that such people are interlopers and therefore unwelcome.This attitude needs to change.

For it is a fact that not enough fieldwork is done where our wildlife is concerned. New-fangled trends and ideas are followed without being adequately thought through while old-fashioned research and fieldwork are neglected. Most forest officers today have jumped into the computer age without studying the actual animal on the ground.

In addition to the lack of systematic, rigorous fieldwork, as I have said elsewhere in this book, another practice I am totally against is human intervention into the world of wild tigers. This excessive interference by man in the tiger's life has taken a toll on the natural balance, impacting on succession and increasing conflict between tigers. Many tigers across India are being kept alive by providing live baits or being fed by baits if they are injured. In one park forest officials went to the extent of pouring water down a cliff from a water tanker in order to create a waterhole near a tigress's den! Some of these interventions are nothing short of ridiculous and stem from ignorance of the tiger. Leave tigers alone. They live and die based on the laws of nature and it is fatal to interfere. I know that in Ranthambhore since 1990 six orphaned cubs were hand-reared on meat and live bait as their mother had been killed or poisoned. As a result, most of these animals became goat lifters and livestock killers. Some had to be airlifted to Sariska. Others created conflict with local villagers and were probably poisoned. I reiterate here that the best policy would be to leave wild tigers alone and not interfere in their life cycle be they adults or cubs. Some will die, others will live. These are the ways of the natural world. Our job is to protect the tiger's turf and not to interfere with its inhabitants. This primary responsibility should never be forgotten as it will determine the tiger's future.

THE FUTURE OF RANTHAMBHORE'S TIGERS

I do not know what the tiger's future will be, but I imagine it will be as stressful as that of the rest of the world. How will tigers survive through all this? This is my thirtieth book but the questions and concerns I raise in it are broadly similar to those I raised in my first book thirty-five years ago.

When discussing the problems thirty-five years ago I wrote: 'A virtual absence of wildlife administration, interdepartmental rivalry, an abundance of boards, bodies and organizations claiming an interest in wildlife, all asserting their influence at various levels without any really serious effort at coordinated action. To top it all, the law and legislation pertaining to the poaching and killing of protected species is totally without teeth. Inordinate delays and a lack of backing from senior officials have made the local guards and wardens wary of tackling poachers who are often backed by local bigwigs.'

On inclusive approaches I said, 'There is no shortcut to involving the people in an effort to protect our wildlife and forests. Some like the Bishnois have traditionally protected animal life—the survival of the black buck in Rajasthan can be largely attributed to their efforts. Others could be motivated. Hunting tribes that live around forest areas could be absorbed in the forest service. With their intimate knowledge of the forest they could become a formidable ally in conserving wildlife.'

On science and research I said, 'There is urgent need for an autonomous body to conduct research on species of animals and birds and their changing relationship with the environment.'

In 1980, in my first book, I emphasized the importance of the persuasive voice of the people and the importance of autonomy. 'The people are those who are concerned about their environment and can create a greater understanding of the tiger, the forest and the meaning of life within it. They have studied the language of the wild and are emotionally tuned to it. These are the ones that must interpret this new language, convincing the administrator of the problems of both plant and animal life, spelling out possible solutions. This effort must be a constant one, a love affair as it were, if this understanding is to grow and transform itself into a reality, crystallizing the thinking of those who make decisions for the forest. Only then can the future of our wilds be secure.'

Today, thirty-six years later, my words would remain the same. My questions are unanswered and still pertinent. All my comments are valid even today. Governments have done more talking than anything else. The machinery for governance is manned by a bureaucracy that does not welcome change even if their political masters support it. That is why little happens and India slowly regresses. I have learnt my lesson in the last four decades and I no longer expect anything from the government. It reveals the sorry state of affairs. We still have not done justice to anything. The forest department has become fatter, richer and more insular. Many senior forest officers have created fiefdoms under them with little concern about good governance or any kind of innovative intervention. The same is true of the politicians around them and it is pertinent to state here that this attitude percolates across the entire sector of our administrative services. Large tracts of forests are gone. Somehow Ranthambhore's tigers are still going on. The credit for that lies with a few forest officers who cared and a very effective NGO engagement which was welcomed on occasion. This combination at critical times saved Ranthambhore from disaster. Fingers crossed, it will continue to do so.

◆

Sometimes I feel that my life in the service of India's wild tigers has been a complete failure. I had dreams of triggering radical reform in wildlife governance but they never came true. However hard I tried the bureaucratic system of governance suffocated all innovation. I have lived with tigers now for forty years. The best part of these years was when I was following tigers in the forests of Ranthambhore. The worst part of these years was when I chased both politicians and bureaucrats to do their jobs in relation to the tigers in their charge. Most of the bureaucrats I encountered were self-serving and uninterested in the tigers' needs. Fortunately there were always a few who acted—the tiny minority that create positive change be they politicians, forest officers, Indian Administrative Service or Indian Police Service officers whom I befriended over the years and learnt much from. Most of them will go unnamed (this is in their own interest) but each one of them will receive a copy of this book as at some level they played a vital role in keeping Ranthambhore's tigers alive. It was in the 1990s that I engaged with both central and state governments campaigning for the tiger's needs and the change necessary to secure its future. This continued for two decades and then my time in the magical forests of Ranthambhore declined. I still found ways to live with my tigers and created a den for myself at home which contains a comprehensive collection of tiger literature and imagery. For me the imagery was inspirational and fought the loneliness and depression I felt being stuck in a city and its dreary corridors of power. Even today I go on battling and engaging in order to serve wild tigers.

I was delighted when some of my initiatives took off in 2015. The Rajasthan government accepted a new scheme that I created called the Van Dhan Yojana, which in effect reduces conflict zones immediately adjacent to wildlife areas and tiger reserves. The pilot project has just been started in the villages adjacent to the Ranthambhore Tiger Reserve. The same government has also accepted my idea of reducing carbon footprints across the state in order to combat climate change and global warming. I also managed to persuade the railway minister of India to accept the idea of the local painters of Ranthambhore repainting the walls of Sawai

Madhopur railway station with murals on tigers and wildlife. The station has now become a remarkable public space with 5,000 square feet of wall paintings that have the look of an open-air art museum. Today the villager, the traveller and hundreds of passengers a day are engaged and entertained by some astounding art and I hope they will increase the awareness to keep Ranthambhore safe and well. I hope the same thing will happen across India at several railway stations where thousands congregate, in order to showcase the cultural and natural heritage of this amazing country. This is the only way to engage the public with what is so precious in this country. Let people breathe in and absorb the beauty of the tiger—that is the best way to save it. In 2016, I have been engaged in the relocation of villages in the corridor that connects Ranthambhore to the adjacent Kela Devi Sanctuary. A new area will open up for the tigers of Ranthambhore to inhabit and in this intervention lies the most important strategy for the future of Ranthambhore's tigers.

Let me end on a positive note—a look at the enduring allure of Ranthambhore's tigers. In the summer of 2016 I witnessed two remarkable incidents involving Ranthambhore's wild tigers that I had never seen before. One involved the sub-adult male cub of T19. He sat under a tree full of fruit bats while a huge dust storm raged. As the branches swayed some bats fell to the ground. The young tiger pounced on them and gobbled them up just like a human child will greedily eat toffees. He ate at least eight of them that afternoon. In Kaziranga National Park tigers are said to wait for young pelicans to fall from their nests in nesting colonies in order to gorge on them.

Then, in June, another young sub-adult spent ten minutes playing with a langur, both slapping each other and chasing each other without the tiger harming the monkey. Another first recorded in Ranthambhore for the chronicles of tiger behaviour. The magic of Ranthambhore lives on.

EPILOGUE

I DECIDED TO FINISH THIS BOOK IN THE PLACE THAT WAS its inspiration, and that had provided much of its content— Ranthambhore. On 31 December 2015, I was in my favourite place in the world—Jogi Mahal in Ranthambhore. Curled up in a chair, time stood still just as it had in the first days I spent there in 1976. I soaked in the peace of the moment. A pied kingfisher hovered above ready to dive-bomb the water for a fish. In the distance an osprey circled the water. Two crocodiles basked on rocks at the edge of the lake sharing their space with a softshell turtle. Across the waters facing me a burst of chital alarm calls had me totally alert—could it be—yes, a young sub-adult male, T19's son, was walking on the far side of the lake. I rushed to my jeep and quickly drove to the other side to observe him walk along the edge of the water, pausing briefly to stalk a couple of crocodiles. After chasing them into the water, he continued his leisurely stroll and vanished into a nullah.

As the year turned, another exceptional surprise awaited me. On 2 January, at 10.30 a.m., on Butterfly Lane I saw an enormous leopard below the arch of an ancient gate. It was least expected and a shock to both leopard and me. It then disappeared but suddenly reappeared in front of us and tiger-like started approaching the jeep with the sun glinting off its head. As it paced forward it sniffed the ground and then started marking the bushes on the road. I was astonished. It was the very first time in forty years that I had witnessed a leopard behaving this way. Normally they are very shy and elusive.

The enchantment of the day did not stop there. As we went on to Rajbagh, T19's female sub-adult daughter was stretched across the road. She soon rose and went to a low-lying tree and clambered on it to rub her cheeks and leave her scent behind. She then ambled into high grass. When we moved on to Malik Talao her sister was at the edge of the lake. Within an hour a young chital moved to the water's edge for a drink and immediately the young tigress went into a crouch and slowly stalked the chital but was noticed. As she raced in, the chital fled. I did not think that she would get it but after a 300-metre chase she downed it and carried it back in her mouth into high grass to feed. Her charge was like a cheetah's and it was the perfect end to an exceptional day.

On one of the following days, I was driving into the non-tourism zone of Lahpur one afternoon when we got a message that a tigress had been seen with two cubs. This was possibly T63, T19's female cub, now nearly five to six years old. And then delight of delights—we found the tigress just off the road with one of her cubs curiously watching the other, exceedingly shy and nervous. They were probably after a drink of water. They led us to the half-eaten carcass of a large spotted deer stag partly hidden in bush and grass. Then just off the road I noticed a dead piglet. The tigress must have killed it while feeding on the deer. It was a tiger's larder. I watched as the cubs, who were barely four months old, played around the spotted deer sinking their tiny teeth into the flesh and bone. In between they would run to the lazing mother for a cuddle and sometimes bump into each other with playful bursts of energy. This was their very first human encounter. The dominant cub, curious and confident, was a female and she finally got the courage to come near us and yank the piglet away. Tiger and piglet were much the same size. Over rock and stone this little cub dragged the piglet until she got near her mother some 12 metres away. It was a tremendous feat and something I had never witnessed amongst cubs of that age. At 5 p.m. we left them to their larder and decided to return the next day at first light. We had a good chance that they would be there. And they were. They were chewing on the spotted deer; the tigress made efforts to drag it away but the legs of the deer got entangled in some branches. The cubs played for a while but as the sun rose the tigress walked off, probably to the water. Her dominant cub followed but changed direction on the road walking up to my jeep and settling down in front of it for a few minutes before following her mother's path. The shy cub raced after her mother. Sambar bellowed in alarm in the distance. I was sure that they would all be back as there were still about 20 kilograms of meat on the deer. For more than an hour nothing happened and then, without warning, I saw the tigress poke her head out of the brush at the edge of the road. She crossed back to the deer. I was sure the cubs would follow but since the tiger always throws a surprise the next moment the tigress had picked up the carcass and in a flash crossed the road and returned to the far side. She was headed to a spot where there were no tracks for jeeps. She had probably deposited her cubs in a safe place and come back alone to carry the carcass to them. An hour later, we found T19's sub-adult daughter at Malik Talao charging the edges of the lake without perfect technique. We watched her for a while and then went back to Jogi Mahal. As I sat on the balcony another tiger exploded from the grass to drink at the lakeside. It had been a feast of tigers. I was overjoyed to see this new generation of tigers in full flight, they reminded of the tigers of the 1980s. I had one more day to go.

My last day was spent in the heart of the tourist zone. I sat by Malik Talao some distance from where T19's female sub-adult crouched in the grass. Sambar, with their penchant for grass that abounds in the water, were at the edges and in the shallow waters of the lake. Every move of theirs was watched by the tigress. At the young age of twenty-one months she had not perfected her hunting technique but shades of Genghis and Noon were evident in her very temperament. After watching the deer for an hour I could see her getting restless. The deer were not near enough for an attack. Yet she suddenly exploded into action. Huge sheets of water soared into the sky and the sambar ran helter-skelter. She raced around them and towards dry land, covering more than 400 metres in repeated charges. A few sambar held their positions watching her closely. The young tigress retraced her steps but again chased the few sambar watching her. The sambar fled. The lake was now completely empty. She scanned the empty lake before moving off into high grass. At that moment I picked up chital calls from a kilometre away—I went off to find her sister sitting on the bank of Rajbagh Lake. I could now hear calls behind me as her sister was on the move to Rajbagh. Tiger activity everywhere. I moved back to find the young tigress pacing down the road and entering the high grass at Rajbagh. The deer fled from her. Her sister on the far side now rose and very purposefully walked down towards her sibling roaring loudly. One of the sisters sat near the backwaters of

Rajbagh. She was alert and I expected a confrontation. Sure enough, in minutes the other tigress arrived and snarled viciously at her sister both rising up to box each other. The smaller tigress submitted by rolling on her back and they quietly moved off into the high grass to rest. This was tiger behaviour that most tiger watchers would give an arm and a leg for.

One striking fact about Ranthambhore's tigers is that they develop relationships with you and vice versa. In my opinion this is because of the very dry forest and excellent visibility. This is why tigers and human beings are able to recognize each other easily and are able to interpret each other's behaviour that otherwise would be impossible. This is why Ranthambhore's tigers have been able to rewrite the natural history of tigers for the world. They were able to remove the veil of secrecy that surrounds wild tigers because of the much more open and accessible forest they live in unlike the tigers in the thicker forests of central and southern India that are difficult to even glimpse. 'Seeing is Believing' and that is why my forty years with Ranthambhore's tigers have been so rewarding.

As I made the return trip to Delhi, I thought about the future of Ranthambhore. It was evident that its tiger population was thriving but would that be the case in the future? What was required was commitment and unsparing effort on the part of wildlife officers and all those concerned with the welfare of tigers in the wild. I have done my bit over four decades but I often ask myself whether I have been able to do anything in all this time that will forever secure the future of wild tigers in India. If I am being completely honest, I do not think I have been successful in my endeavour. Yes, due to efforts of exceptional forest officers like Fateh, G. V. Reddy, now the chief wildlife warden of Rajasthan, and Shree Bhagwan, now the chief wildlife warden of Maharashtra, wildlife reserves like Ranthambhore and Tadoba Tiger Reserve in Maharashtra have succeeded in becoming tiger havens. It is because of people like them as well as bureaucrats like Praveen Pardeshi, who is presently principal secretary to the chief minister of Maharashtra, that I believe that there is still some hope left for the wild tigers of India.

But if these magnificent creatures are going to delight our children's children we will need to come up with innovative solutions, and genuine workable initiatives between governments, non-governmental organizations and private companies. At the moment, dedicated men like G.V. Reddy, Shree Bhagwan, Ajit Singh Shekhawat, Giriraj Singh Kushwaha, Nihal Chand Goel and Praveen Pardeshi are few and far between, we need scores more like them who are supported with funds and government initiatives so the wild tigers of Ranthambhore and other reserves in the country can continue to flourish.

ACKNOWLEDGEMENTS

There are many people from all walks of life who played critical roles over the past forty years in the growth and success of Ranthambhore and every one of them has my deepest appreciation. It would have been impossible for me to write about tigers over a period of four decades unless the park was well protected and defended. That this book was able to come about was because several people had a role to play.

First and most importantly, I must thank my family—my parents Raj and Romesh Thapar, who were with me as my first decade in Ranthambhore unfolded. They respected my endeavours even though this was a subject completely alien to them. I introduced them to wild tigers and their unfailing support of me, until they passed away in 1987, deserves special mention. My sister Malvika Singh encouraged and promoted all my engagements with Ranthambhore and provided unstinting support and continues to do so. I have no words to thank her. I am equally grateful to her husband Tejbir, with whom I spent more than twelve years, from 1976 onwards trying to record the secret life of tigers. I am just as indebted to my aunt Romila Thapar, who gave me little nuggets of unique information that formed the historical perspective to whatever I wrote. Over the last twenty years my wife Sanjna Kapoor has played a pivotal role by supporting and encouraging me during my most frustrating moments dealing with India's depressing bureaucracy. Her energy and warmth are truly inspiring. My nephew Jaisal Singh and his wife Anjali have played a vital role over the past decade by ensuring that Ranthambhore has got the attention it deserved. Above all, my son Hamir, who has grown up with me in the amazing world of Ranthambhore—I have few words to describe not just the delight but also the inspiration this provided me to go on battling in whatever way necessary for Ranthambhore.

One of the key players in the Ranthambhore success story was Vasundhara Raje, the present chief minister of Rajasthan. I did not know her well but, thanks to my sister Malvika, I met her in 1991-92 and she played a vital role when the first poaching scandal blew up in Ranthambhore. Vasundhara Raje arranged for me to meet the then chief minister of Rajasthan, Bhairon Singh Shekhawat, and did this on several occasions in order to find solutions to the crisis. In fact, in 1992, I was invited to address a meeting of senior bureaucrats in the chief minister's office in Jaipur to find solutions to secure Ranthambhore's future. At the turn of the century, when Vasundhara Raje herself was chief minister, she created an empowered committee to deal with the second crisis that took place in Sariska Tiger Reserve and Ranthambhore. During both her tenures she has played an essential role in taking correct decisions at the right time, where wildlife conservation is concerned. She still believes in keeping tigers safe. As chief minister today she has created a standing committee to monitor and implement innovative decisions. God alone knows what would have happened without her timely actions and immediate responses.

It is remarkable how Ranthambhore has enjoyed

positive political support from both the principal parties, the Congress and the Bharatiya Janata Party. Its national and global impact commands the attention of one and all. As prime ministers Rajiv Gandhi, I. K. Gujral and Dr Manmohan Singh were willing to support Ranthambhore. Rajiv Gandhi and his family spent one unforgettable week there in 1986 and the impact of that visit still remains. Sonia Gandhi as chairperson of the UPA was always ready to support good interventions in this landscape. Manmohan Singh came to Ranthambhore after the poaching scandals of 2005, spent a night on the edges of the forest, and even saw a tiger. Kamal Nath and Suresh Prabhu, as ministers of environment and forests, were always willing to give their support. In fact, as rail minister in 2016, Suresh Prabhu supported my idea to paint the walls of Sawai Madhopur Station so it became a living art museum full of the images of Ranthambhore's tigers. Jairam Ramesh, whom I had known for many years, was also exciting to talk to while he was minister but my greatest disappointment was his inability to keep bureaucrats at arm's length.

From my very first decade in Ranthambhore I realized that the dedication and perseverance of the forest staff were vital to the park's success. One of the first to acknowledge this was a man called Kailash Sankhala from the Rajasthan forest cadre who was the first director of Project Tiger in Delhi in its formative years (1974). He loved Ranthambhore and was directly responsible for including this area in the first nine tiger reserves ever declared. Later he became chief wildlife warden of Rajasthan and continued to promote and strengthen Ranthambhore. He was a source of great inspiration for Fateh Singh who was my tiger guru and the man who built Ranthambhore and made it the most exciting destination in the world for tigers.

During my first two decades I was deeply involved with forest staff, workers and the first guides and jeep drivers—Prahlad, Laddu, Dharma, Chotu, Chitar, Badhyaya, Ramu, Ramesh, Bahadur, Gaffar, Abhay, Daulat, Manohar, Mahinder, Manoj, Ranjit, Saeed, Dharam Singh, Mohan Singh, Phul Chand and many others including the first taxi drivers and guides—Shafiq, Nafees, Shamim, Salim and many more with whom I spent time watching the secrets of tigers unfold. By 1988, Fateh's son, Goverdhan Singh Rathore, engaged with me to set up the Ranthambhore Foundation and then at the turn of the century created his own health centre, school and now a hospital for the people of Sawai Madhopur. He continues his pursuits outside the park with an unmatched zeal and with the aim of protecting tigers.

Just before the turn of the century, when Ranthambhore faced a serious set of problems, forest officer G. V. Reddy took over as director of Ranthambhore and we worked together in a rare harmony. His presence was an essential element in keeping Ranthambhore safe at this time.

There were many others who worked closely with Ranthambhore Foundation's ideas to reduce the conflict between the park and people. Both Paola Manfredi and Peter Lawton and their inputs were indispensable throughout the 1990s. Shamji, Nitin, Ujwala, Nagina, Jagan Sarpanch and many others were part of a team that fought endless battles to preserve and protect Ranthambhore's treasures.

During the last fifteen years the work of

Ranthambhore's army has continued. Geoff and Diane Ward have done their very best to support Ranthambhore. So have Iskander Laljee and John and Faith Singh. Dharmendra Khandal spearheads Tiger Watch and is a dedicated field biologist who with his innovative ideas brings great strength to Ranthambhore's forests. Michael Birkhead brought the power of film and the media to reflect the problems of Ranthambhore at critical times for the world to see. His support of me to anchor his television programmes about Ranthambhore's tigers is deeply appreciated. Today, many continue to fight the battle to ensure that Ranthambhore lives. Y. K. Sahu, the present field director and his vital and timely inputs, Sudarshan Sharma, Aditya 'Dicky' Singh, R. S. Shekhawat, Balendu Singh, R. S. Kala, Daulat Singh are only a few that deserve mention.

Indian Administrative Service officers like Salauddin Ahmed, Indian Police Service officers like Shantanu Kumar and Ajit Singh Shekhawat, played pivotal roles at different times in Ranthambhore's history. Alok Vashistha and Samir Kumar Singh, both police officers, played strategic roles in anti-poaching drives. Relationships with both government officers and politicians are bumpy at the best of times. Some who deserve mention are Bina Kak, V. D. Sharma, R. G. Soni, the late B. L. Meena, Tejveer Singh, G. S. Bharadwaj, and Rahul Bhatnagar. A bunch of non-governmental organizations, both national and international, supported different initiatives in the park. These include the World Wide Fund for Nature, Centre for Environmental Education, Dastkar, Prakratik Society, the Ranthambhore School of Art and master painters such as Immamudin, Narayan Singh, Gajanand Singh and M. D. Parashar, Tiger

Watch, Wildlife Conservation Trust, Intach (Indian National Trust for Art and Cultural Heritage), BAIF (Bharatiya Agro Industries Foundation), Global Tiger Patrol, Care for the Wild, and the David Shepherd Wildlife Foundation. Many others engaged in smaller ways. The Wildlife Institute of India and K. Ullas Karanth conducted some vital scientific studies of tigers.

A host of individuals from across India and the world gave their support and continue to do so. M. K. Jiwrajka, in his role as member secretary of the Centrally Empowered Committee set up by the Supreme Court of India, was always there to provide strategic support to prevent any abuse of the habitat. P. K. Sen, the very dynamic former director of Project Tiger, Bharat Kapoor, Bittu Sahgal, Amanda Bright, Belinda Wright, Ravi Singh, Mahendra Vyas and Yusuf Ansari added their strengths to the cause of Ranthambhore. More recently, V. P. Singh, Anshu Jain and Hemendra Kothari provided great assistance. VP ran a very dynamic empowered committee that played a vital role to keep Ranthambhore safe at the turn of the century. The forest department over two decades received dozens of vehicles and motorcycles; the forest staff welfare society got free guidebooks to sell; countless jackets, sweaters and kits were distributed to forest staff; various life insurance and accident insurance schemes were set up for them and new forest chowkis were sponsored. The aim was to leave no stone unturned towards the cause of keeping Ranthambhore protected and well-funded.

Many journalists played their part, including Jay Mazoomdaar, who in 2005 broke the story of the extinction of tigers in Sariska. *Sanctuary* magazine relayed

Ranthambhore's stories to wider audiences across India. The crisis of the moment immediately made it to the pages of both local and national newspapers; the well-wishers of Ranthambhore began to number in the millions.

An amazing interdisciplinary effort supports the very fabric of Ranthambhore even though most of the time it is not organized. Whether we like to believe it or not we are like a part of Fateh's army all sharing one common thread—our love for Ranthambhore and wanting to do something more for its welfare—irrespective of how that intervention might be judged later. In August 2016, G. V. Reddy is the new dynamic chief wildlife warden, and Ajit Singh Shekhawat, now DG of police, is the chair of a standing committee on wildlife that reports to Chief Minister Vasundhara Raje. Giriraj Singh Kushwaha, a remarkable civil servant, and myself, also serve this committee. Dharmendra Khandal is an asset to this committee and plays a critical role in keeping Ranthambhore safe. And so the battle to protect Ranthambhore goes on.

I have probably missed out many names of those who struggled for Ranthambhore over the decades but I am sure the tigers of Ranthambhore will be ever grateful for their efforts. It is important to record all the above so that the public at large realizes the enormous amount of work that goes in to keep a tiger landscape alive. Such interventions have happened in many other places too and I hope the younger generation will continue to engage in securing the future of amazing landscapes such as Ranthambhore.

◆

In regard to the book you have just read, there are a few

people I wish to thank. I have to thank David Davidar, co-founder of Aleph Book Company, for coming up with the idea for this book. 'You've written twenty-nine books,' he said to me one day, 'but there is not one that has all your favourite tigers and your best encounters in one volume. Do it for posterity and keep it simple.' And that is what I have tried to do in this book, reliving the very best of my experiences with Ranthambhore's tigers.

I must thank the designer Bena Sareen for the cover and text design and I must thank the entire Aleph team for producing a superb book.

BIBLIOGRAPHY

Ahmad, Shahbaz, *The Crisis of the Tiger*, Maryland: American Star Books, 2009.

Aitken, Edward Hamilton, *A Naturalist on the Prowl*, Calcutta: Thacker, Spink, 1897.

Allen, Hugh, *The Lonely Tiger*, London: Faber and Faber, 1960.

Alvi, M. A., and Rahman, A., *Jahangir: The Naturalist*, Delhi: Indian National Science Academy, 1968.

Amore, C., *20 Ways to Track a Tiger*, U.S.A.: Wildlife Worlds, 2003.

Antón, Mauricio, *Sabertooth*, Bloomington: Indiana University Press, 2013.

Archer, Milfred, *Tippoo's Tiger*, London: Victoria and Albert Museum, 1959.

Baikov, N. A., *The Manchurian Tiger: Big Game Hunting in Manchuria*, London: Hutchinson, 1925/1936.

Baker, S., *Wild Beasts and Their Ways*, London: Macmillan, 1891.

Banerjee, Ananda, *Nature Chronicles of India: Essays on Wildlife*, New Delhi: Rupa Publications India, 2014.

Barnes, Simon, *Tiger!* London: Boxtree, 1994.

Barras, J., *India and Tiger-hunting*, London: W. Swan Sonnenschein & Co, 1885.

———, *The New Shikari at Our Indian Stations*, London: W. Swan Sonnenschein & Co, 1885.

Bazé, William, *Tiger! Tiger!* London: Elek Books, 1957.

Bedi, Rajesh, and Bedi, Ramesh, *Indian Wildlife*, New Delhi: Brijbasi, 1984.

Bennet, E. T., *The Tower Menagerie*, London: Robert Jennings, 1829.

Berg, B. M., *Tiger and Mensch*, Berlin: Halltorp, 1934.

Bergmann Sucksdorff, A., *Tiger in Sight*, London: André Deutsch, 1970.

Best, J. W., *Forest Life in India*, London: John Murray, 1935.

———, *Indian Shikar Notes*, London: John Murray, 1922.

———, *Tiger Days*, London: John Murray, 1931.

Bharadwaj, Gobind Sagar, *Tracking Tigers in Ranthambhore*, Noida: Aureole Publishers, 2008.

Bond, Ruskin, *Shikar Stories: 7 Great Animal Stories*, New Delhi: Rupa Publications, 2010.

Boomgaard, P., *Frontiers of Fear*, London: Yale University Press, 2001.

Booth, Martin, *Carpet Sahib: A Life of Jim Corbett*, London: Constable, 1986.

Boyes, Jonathan, *Tiger-men and Tofu Dolls: Tribal Spirits in Northern Thailand*, Chiang Mai: Silkworm Books, 1997.

Braddon, E., *Thirty Years of Shikar*, London: William Blackwood and Sons, 1895.

Bradley, M. H., *Trailing the Tiger*, New York: D. Appleton, 1929.

Breeden, Stanley, and Wright, Belinda, *Through the Tiger's Eyes: A Chronicle of India's*

Wildlife, Berkeley: Ten Speed Press, 1996.

Brown, J. M., *Shikar Sketches: With Notes on Indian Field-Sports*, London: Hurst and Blackett, 1887.

Brunskill, C., *Tiger Forest: A Visual Study of Ranthambhore National Park*, London: Troubador, 2003.

Burke, W. S., *The Indian Field Shikar Book*, London: Thacker, Spink & Co, 1920.

Burton, R. G., *Sport and Wild Life in the Deccan*, London: Seeley, Service & Co, 1928.

———, *The Book of the Tiger*, London: Hutchinson, 1933.

———, *The Tiger Hunters*, London: Hutchinson, 1936.

Caldwell, H. R., *Blue Tiger*, London: Duckworth, 1925.

Campbell, Danny, *The Last of the Siamese Tigers*, CreateSpace Independent Publishing Platform, 2014.

Campbell, W., *The Old Forest Ranger*, London: How and Parsons, 1842.

Chakrabarti, Kalyan, *Man-eating Tigers*, Calcutta: Darbari Prokashan, 1992.

Chalise, Lina, *Royal Bengal Tiger: Panthera Tigris Tigris in Nepal*, Saarbrücken: (LAP) Lambert Academic Publishing, 2012.

Champion, F. W., *The Jungle in Sunlight and Shadow*, London: Chatto and Windus, 1925.

———, *With a Camera in Tiger-land*, London: Chatto and Windus, 1927.

———, *Tripwire for a Tiger*, Chennai: Rain Fed Books, 2012.

Corbett, Jim, *Man-eaters of Kumaon*, Oxford: Oxford University Press, 1944.

Choudhary, L. K., and Khan, S. A., *Bandhavgarh Fort of the Tiger*, Bhopal: Sandhya Prakash Bhavan, 2003.

Choudhury, Khairi, S. R., *The Beloved Tigress*, Dehradun: Natraj, 1999.

Courtney, N., *The Tiger, Symbol of Freedom*, London: Quartet Books, 1980.

Cubitt, Gerald, and Mountfort, Guy, *Wild India*, London: Collins, 1985.

Daniel, J. C., *The Tiger in India: A Natural History*, Dehradun: Natraj, 2003.

Davidar, E. R. C., *Whispers from the Wild*, New Delhi: Penguin India, 2012.

Denzau, Gertrude, and Denzau, Helmut, *Königstiger*, Steinfurt: Teclenborg Verlag, 1996.

Elliott, J. G., *Field Sports in India, 1800-1947*, London: Gentry Books, 1973.

Digby, G. B., *Tigers, Gold, and Witchdoctors*, New York: Harcourt Brace, 1928.

Eardley-Wilmot, S., *Forest Life and Sport in India*, London: Edward Arnold, 1910.

———, *The Life of a Tiger*, London: Ames, 1911.

Ellis, Richard, *Tiger Bone and Rhino Horn: The Destruction of Wildlife for Traditional Chinese Medicine*, Washington D. C.: Shearwater Books, 2005.

Ellison, Bernard, *The Prince of Wales in India*, London: Heinemann, 1925.

Evans, G. P., *Big-Game Shooting in Upper Burma*, London: Longmans, Green, 1912.

Zimmerman, F., *The Jungle and the Aroma of Meats*, Columbia: South Asia Books, 1999.

Fayrer, J., *The Royal Tiger of Bengal: His Life and Death*, London: J. and A. Churchill, 1875.

Felix, *Recollections of a Bison and Tiger Hunter,* London: J. M. Dent, 1906.

Fend, Werner, *Die Tiger von Abutschmar*, Vienna: Verlag Fritz Molden, 1972.

Fife-Cookson, Colonel J. C., *Tiger Shooting in the Doon and Ulwar*, London: Chapman and Hall, 1887.

Fletcher, W. F., *Sport in the Nilgiris and in Wynaad*, London: Macmillan, 1911.

Forbes, James, *Oriental Memoirs*, 2 Vols, London: R. Bentley, 1834-1835.

Forrest, Denys, *The Tiger of Mysore: The Life and Death of Tipu Sultan*, London: Chatto and Windus, 1970.

Forsyth. J., *The Highlands of Central India*, London: Chapman and Hall, 1889.

Gee, E. P., *The Wildlife of India*, London: Collins, 1964.

Ghorpade, M.Y., *Sunlight and Shadows*, London: Gollancz, 1983.

Glasfurd, A. I. R., *Musings of an Old Shikari*, London: John Lane and Bodley Head, 1928.

Gomille, Axel, *India: Land of Tigers and Temples*, New Delhi: Bloomsbury India, 2016.

Gopal, Rajesh, *Fundamentals of Wildlife Management*, New Delhi: Natraj Publishers, 2011.

———, *Land of the Striped Stalker*, New Delhi: Wisdom Tree, 2009.

Goswami, Anjali and Friscia, Anthony, *Carnivoran Evolution*, New Delhi: Cambridge University Press, 2010.

Gouldsbury, C. E., *Tiger Slayer by Order*, New York: G. Bell and Sons, 1915.

———, *Tigerland*, London: Chapman and Hall, 1913.

Green, Iain, *Wild Tigers of Bandhavgarh—Encounters in a Fragile Forest*, United Kingdom: Tiger Books, 2002.

Gurang, K. K., *Heart of the Jungle: The Wildlife of Chitwan, Nepal*, London: André Deutsch, 1983.

Green, Susie, *Tiger*, London: Reaktion Books, 2006.

Hamilton, D., *Records of Sport in Southern India*, London: R. H. Porter, 1892.

Hanley, P. D., *Tiger Trails in Assam*, London: Robert Hale, 1960.

Harris, H. A., *Sport in Greece and Rome*, London: Thames and Hudson, 1972.

Hayward, Matt, W. and Somers, Michael, *Reintroduction of Top Order*, Hoboken: Wiley-Blackwell, 2009.

Hewett, J. P., *Jungle Trails in Northern India*, London: Metheun, 1938.

Hicks, F. C., *Forty Years among the Wild Animals of India, from Mysore to the Himalayas*, Allahabad: Pioneer Press, 1910.

Hingston, W. G. and Stevens, G. R., *The Tiger Kills*, London: Ames, 1944.

Hodges-Hill, Edward, *Man Eater: Tales of Lion and Tiger Encounters*, London: Cockbird Press, 1992.

Hornaday, W. T., *Two Years in the Jungle*, New York : Charles Scribner's Sons, 1885.

Hornocker, M., *Track of the Tiger*, San Francisco: Sierra Club Books, 1997.

Israel, Samuel, and Sinclair, Toby, *Indian Wildlife*, Singapore: Apa Publications, 1987.

Ives, Richard, *Of Tigers and Men*, New York: Doubleday, 1996.

Jackson, Peter, *Endangered Species: Tiger*, London: Apple Press, 1990.

Jain, Naitik, *My Wildlife Odyssey: A Photographic Journey*, The Write Place, 2015.

Jalais, Annu, *Forest of Tigers: People, Politics and Environment in the Sundarbans*, New Delhi: Routledge India, 2009

Jepson, Stanley, *Big Game Encounters*, London: H. F. & G. Witherby Ltd., 1936.

Johnsingh, AJT and Manjrekar, Neema, *Mammals of South Asia*, New Delhi: Orient Blackswan, 2013.

Johnson, D., *Sketches of Indian Field Sports*, London: Robert Jennings, 1827.

Jung, S., *Tryst with Tigers*, London: Robert Hale, 1967.

Karanth, Ullas, *The Science of Saving Tigers*, New Delhi: Orient Blackswan, 2011.

———, *Two Tiger Tales*, New Delhi: Penguin India, 2016.

Khan, H. Monirul, *Tigers in the Mangroves: Research and Conservation of the Tiger in the Sundarbans of Bangladesh*, Dhaka: Bangla Academy, 2011.

Lanz. J. Tobias, *The Life and Fate of the India Tiger*, Santa Barbara: Greenwood Press, 2009.

Lindblad, Jan, *Tigrata—Vart storsta aventyr*, Belgium: 1982.

Lipton, Mimi, *The Tiger Rugs of Tibet*, London: Thames and Hudson, 1998.

Locke, A, *The Tigers of Trengganu*, London: Museum Press, 1954.

Maharajah of Cooch Behar, *Thirty-Seven Years of Big Game Shooting in Cooch Behar, the Duars, and Assam: A Rough Diary*, Prescott: Wolfe, 1993 (originally published in 1908).

Mandal, Malalay and Roy, Ankita, *Wild Escapades Around Central India*, Resurrect Books, 2016.

Manfredi, Paola, *In Danger: Habitats, Species, and People*, New Delhi: Ranthambhore Foundation, 1997.

Matthiessen, Peter, *Tigers in the Snow*, New York: North Point Press, 2001.

McDougal, Charles, *The Face of the Tiger*, London: Rivington Books, 1977.

McNeely, Jeffrey A., and Wachtel, P. S., *The Soul of the Tiger*, New York: Doubleday, 1988.

Meacham, Cory, *How the Tiger Lost Its Stripes*, New York: Harcourt Brace, 1997.

Mehta, Nita, *Spirit of the Tiger*, New Delhi: Parragon, 2015.

Mills, J. A., *Blood of the Tiger: A Story of Conspiracy, Greed, and the Battle to Save a Magnificent Species*, Boston: Beacon Press, 2015.

Milse, Thorsten and Henschel, Uta, *The Eyes of the Jungle*, Munich: CJ Bucker Verlag, 2008.

Mishra, Hemanta, *Bones of the Tiger: Of Man-Eating Tigers and Tiger-Eating Men*, New Delhi: Penguin India, 2013.

Mockler-Ferryman, A. F., *The Life Story of a Tiger*, London: Adam and Charles Black, 1910.

Montgomery, Sy, *Spell of the Tiger: The Man-eaters of Sundarbans*, Vermont: Chelsea Green Publishing Company, 2009.

Mountfort, Guy, *Back from the Brink*, London: Hutchinson, 1978.

———, *Saving the Tiger*, London: Michael Joseph, 1981.

———, *Tigers*, London: Newton Abbot, 1973.

Mundy, Captain G. C., *Pen and Pencil Sketches, Being the Journal of a Tour in India*, London: John Murray, 1833.

Naidu, M. Kamal, *Trail of the Tiger*, Dehradun: Natraj, 1998.

Niyogi, Tushar K., *Tiger Cult of the Sundarbans*, Calcutta: Anthropological Survey of India, 1996.

Nobis, Bobi, *On Safari: The Tiger and The Baobab Tree*, New Delhi: Om Publications, 2011.

Pabla, H. S., *Road to Nowhere: Wildlife Conservation in India*, CreateSpace Independent Publishing Platform, 2015.

Padel, Ruth, *Tigers in Red Weather*, London: Little Brown Group, 2006.

Panwar, H. S., *Kanha National Park*, London: Cassell, 1964.

Park, Sooyong, *The Great Soul of Siberia*, Vancouver: Greystone Books, 2016.

Peissel, Michel, *Tiger for Breakfast: The Story of Boris of Kathmandu*, New York: Dutton, 1966.

Perry, Richard, *The World of the Tiger*, London: Cassell, 1964.

Prater, S. H., *The Book of Indian Animals*, Bombay: BNHS, 1988.

Quammen, David, *Monster of God: The Man-eating Predator in the Jungles of History and the Mind*, New York: W. W. Norton & Company, 2004.

Quan, Li, *Rewilded: Saving the South China Tiger*, London: Evans Mitchell Books, 2011.

Rabinowitz, Alan, *Chasing the Dragon's Tail*, New York: Doubleday, 1991.

———, *Life in the Valley of Death: The Fight to Save Tigers in a Land of Guns, Gold, and Greed*, Washington D. C.: Island Press, 2010.

Rangarajan, M., *India's Wildlife History*, New Delhi: Permanent Black, 2001.

Ranjitsinh, M. K., *Beyond the Tiger: Portraits of South-Asian Wildlife*, New Delhi: Brijbasi, 1997.

Reid, M., *The Tiger-hunter*, New York: G. W. Dillingham, 1892.

Rice, W., *Indian Game (from Quail to Tiger)*, London: W. H. Allen, 1884.

———, *Tiger-shooting in India*, London: Smith, Elder, 1857.

Rouse, Andy, *Tigers: A Celebration of Life*, Electric Squirrel Publishing, 2010.

Rousselet, L., *The King of the Tigers*, London: S. Low, Marston, Searle and Rivington, 1888.

Sanderson, G. P., *Thirteen Years Among the Wild Beasts of India*, London: W. H. Allen, 1882.

Rupani, Bob, *Tracking the Tiger: 50 days in India's Best Tiger Reserves*, Rupani Media, 2014.

Sankhala, K., *Tiger Land*, New York: Bobbs-Merrill, 1975.

———, *Tiger!* London: Collins, 1978.

Schaller, G. B., *The Deer and the Tiger*, Chicago: University of Chicago Press, 1967.

Scindia, Madhav Rao, *A Guide to Tiger Shooting*, 1920.

Seidensticker, John, Christie, Sarah, and Jackson, Peter, *Riding the Tiger*, Cambridge: Cambridge University Press, 1999.

Sellar, M. John, *The UN's Lone Ranger: Combating International Wildlife Crime*, Caithness: Whittles Publishing, 2014.

Shah, Anup, and Shah, Manoj, *A Tiger's Tale*, Kingston-upon-Thames: Fountain Press, 1996.

Sharma, H. S., *Ranthambhore Sanctuary: Dilemma of Eco Development*, New Delhi: Concept Publishing Company, 2000.

Sharma, Sunayan, *Sariska: The Tiger Reserve Roars Again*, New Delhi: Niyogi Books, 2015.

Singh, Aditya Dicky and Devasar, Nikhil, *Spirit of the Tiger*, New Delhi: Parragon Publishing India, 2012.

Singh, Anjali and Jaisal, Gandhi, Priyanka, *Ranthambhore: The Tiger's Realm*, New Delhi: Sujan Art Pvt Ltd, 2011.

Singh, Bhagat, *Wild Encounters*, New Delhi: Pelican Creations International, 1999.

Singh, Billy Arjan, *Tara, a Tigress*, London: Quartet Books, 1981.

————, *The Legend of the Maneater*, New Delhi: Ravi Dayal, 1993.

————, *Tiger Book*, Delhi: Lotus Roli, 1997.

————, *Tiger Haven*, London: Macmillan, 1973.

————, *A Tiger's Story*, Delhi: HarperCollins, 1999.

————, *Tiger! Tiger!* London: Jonathan Cape, 1984.

Singh, Dr L. S. Tara, *The Cocktail Tigress: The Story of Genetic Pollution of the Indian Tigers*, Allahabad: Print World, 2000.

Singh, K., *One Man and a Thousand Tigers*, New York: Dodd, Mead: 1959.

————, *The Tiger of Rajasthan*, London: Robert Hale, 1959.

Singh, V., and Shrivastava, A.K., *Biodiversity of Ranthambhore Tiger Reserve Rajasthan*, Jodhpur: Scientific Publishers, 2007.

Sinha, V. R., *The Tiger is a Gentleman*, Bangalore: Wildlife, 1999.

Smythies, E. A., *Big Game Shooting in Nepal*, Calcutta: Thacker, Spink, 1942.

Smythies, O., *Tiger Lady*, London: Heinemann, 1953.

Stacton, David, *A Ride on a Tiger*, London: Museum Press, 1954.

Stebbing, E. P., *Jungle By-ways in India*, London: John Lane and Bodley Head, 1911.

————, *The Diary of a Sportsman Naturalist in India*, London: John Lane, 1920.

Stewart, A. E., *Tiger and Other Game*, London: Longman's, Green, 1878.

Stracey, P. D., *Tigers*, London: Arthur Barker, 1968.

Sukumar, Raman, *The Story of Asia's Elephants*, Mumbai: Marg Publications, 2011.

Sunquist, Fiona, and Sunquist, Mel, *Tiger Moon*, Chicago: University of Chicago Press, 1988.

————, *Wild Cats of the World*, Chicago: University of Chicago 2002.

Sutton, R. L., *Tiger Trails in Southern Asia*, St. Louis: C.V. Mosby, 1926.

Taraporewala, Soonoo, *Tiger Warrior: Fateh Singh Rathore of Ranthambhore*, New Delhi: Penguin India, 2012.

Taylor, M. L., *The Tiger's Claw*, London: Burke, 1956.

Thapar, Romila, *Early India, From the Origins to A.D. 1300*, Berkeley: University of California Press, 2003.

————, *From Lineage to State*, New York: Oxford University Press, 1985.

Thapar, Valmik, *An African Diary: 12 Days in Kenya's Magical Wilderness*, New Delhi: Oxford University Press, 2009.

————, *Bridge of God: 20 Days in the Masai Mara*.

————, *Battling for Survival: India's Wilderness over Two Centuries*, New Delhi: Oxford University Press, 2003.

————, *Saving Wild Tigers*, New Delhi: Oxford University Press, 2001.

————, with Thapar, Romila and Ansari, Yusuf, *Exotic Aliens*, New Delhi: Aleph Book Company, 2013.

————, *My Life with Tigers*, New Delhi: Oxford University Press, 2013.

————, *Ranthambhore: 10 Days in the Tiger Fortress*, New Delhi: Oxford University

Press, 2008.

————, *Saving Wild India: A Blueprint for Change,* New Delhi: Aleph Book Company, 2015.

————, *The Illustrated Tigers of India,* New Delhi: Oxford University Press, 2007.

————, *The Last Tiger,* New Delhi: Oxford University Press, 2011.

————, *The Tiger: Soul of India,* New Delhi: Oxford University Press, 2010.

————, *Tiger Fire: 500 Years of the Tiger in India,* New Delhi: Aleph Book Company, 2014.

————, *Tiger: The Ultimate Guide,* New York: CDS Books, 2004.

————, *Tigers and the Banyan Tree,*

————, *Tigers and Tigerwallahs* with Jim Corbett, Billy Arjan Singh, Geoffrey C. Ward and Diane Raines Ward, New Delhi: Oxford University Press, 2002.

————, *Tigers in the Emerald Forest: Ranthambhore after the Monsoon,* New Delhi: Oxford University Press, 2012.

————, *Tigers, My Life: Ranthambhore and Beyond,* New Delhi: Oxford University Press, 2011.

————, *Wild Fire: The Splendours of India's Animal Kingdom,* New Delhi: Aleph Book Company, 2015.

————, *Winged Fire: A Celebration of Indian Birds,* New Delhi: Aleph Book Company, 2016.

————, *Battling for Survival,* New Delhi: Oxford University Press, 2003.

————, *The Cult of the Tiger,* New Delhi: Oxford University Press, 2002.

————, *The Land of the Tiger,* London: BBC Books, 1997.

————, *The Secret Life of Tigers,* New Delhi: Oxford University Press, 1998.

————, *Tiger: Habitats, Life Cycle, Food Chains, and Threats,* London: Wayland, 1999.

————, *The Tiger's Destiny,* London: Kyle Cathie, 1992.

————, *Tiger: Portrait of a Predator,* London: Collins, 1986.

————, *Tigers: The Secret Life,* London: Hamish Hamilton, 1989.

————, *Wild Tigers of Ranthambhore,* New Delhi: Vikas Publishing, 1983.

————, *With Tigers in the Wild,* New Delhi: Vikas Publishing, 1983.

Tilson, R., and Seal, U., *Tigers of the World: The Biology, Biopolitics, Management, and Conservation of an Endangered Species.* Park Ridge: Noyes Publications, 1987.

Todd, W. H., *Tiger! Tiger!* London: Heath Cranton, 1927.

Toovey, J., *Tigers of the Raj,* Gloucester: Alan Sutton, 1987.

Trench, Philip, *Tiger Hunting: A Day's Sport in the East,* London: Hodgson and Graves, 1836.

Turner, Alan, *The Big Cats and Their Fossil Relatives,* New York: Columbia University Press, 1997.

Tyabji, Hashim, *Bandhavgarh National Park,* New Delhi: 1994.

Vaillant, John, *The Tiger: A True Story of Vengeance & Survival,* London: Vintage, 2011.

Verma, Som Prakash, *Flora and Fauna of Mughal Art,* Mumbai: Marg Publications, 1999.

Vogel, Julia, *Tigers: Built for the Hunt,* Mankato: Capstone Press, 2015.

Ward, Geoffrey C. with Ward, Diane Raines, *Tiger Wallahs: Encounters with the Men*

Who Tried to Save the Great Cats, New York: HarperCollins, 1993.

Wardrop, Major A. E., *Days and Nights of Indian Big Game*, London: Macmillan, 1923.

Winter, Steve, *Tigers Forever: Saving the World's Most Endangered Big Cat*, National Geographic, 2013.

Yudakov, Anatoliy Grigorievitch and Nikolaev, Georgievitch Igor, *The Ecology of the Amur Tiger based on Long-Term Winter Observations in 1970-1973 in the Western Sector of the Central Sikhote-Alin Mountains*, Moscow: Nauka Publishers, 1987.

Zanjale, Anant, *Portrait of Wild India*, New Delhi: Partridge India, 2015.

Zwaenepoel, Jean-Pierre, *Tigers*, San Francisco: Chronicle Books, 1992.

www.ingramcontent.com/pod-product-compliance
Lightning Source LLC
Chambersburg PA
CBHW030931150426
42812CB00064B/2742/J